Hidden Treasures in Plain Sight

By
VELMA HAGAR

Copyright © 2025 by Velma Hagar. All rights reserved.

No part of this book can be used or reproduced in any manner whatsoever without written permission from the author except as provided by the United States of America copyright law or in the case of brief quotations embodied in articles and reviews.

Disclaimer: References to Scripture are the author's paraphrase.
Cover Photo: Stacey Mills

Paperback: ISBN: 978-0-9981828-5-8
eBook ISBN: 978-0-9981828-6-5

Published in the United States of America

Printed in the United States of America.

Introduction

MY NEWEST BOOK, *Hidden Treasures in Plain Sight*, comes with a revelation that feels both exciting and long overdue. It dawned on me that not all hidden treasures are tucked away in secret or dark places. Many treasures are right out in the open—plain as day—but often go unnoticed.

My first two books, *Hidden Treasures in Secret Places* and *Hidden Treasures in Dark Places*, have been so well-received, earning five-star reviews and touching countless lives. Many readers have asked, "When will the next book be coming?" I kept brushing it off, saying, "I'm too old!" And let's face it—82 is no spring chicken. But here I am, writing every day, brimming with energy, joy, and gratitude for my good health. Not to mention, my hair is still naturally black! (A little vanity never hurt anyone.)

So, with renewed enthusiasm, I present the third book in my *Hidden Treasures* series. This one takes a fresh approach, uncovering the treasures that are hiding in plain sight.

At the beginning of each month's chapter, you'll find a foreword written by my children and some of my grandchildren. Through their words and heartfelt reflections on "Bubby"—their affectionate name for me—you'll get an intimate glimpse into my life, as seen through their eyes.

My deepest prayer is that you'll not only enjoy reading this book but that it will also be life changing. May it teach you to recognize and embrace the treasures in your life, whether they're hidden in dark places, secret places, or lying right in plain sight.

BUBBY HAS ALWAYS been proud to say that I take after her...We both love to yap, love to dance and are naturally very flexible, and we love to laugh and be silly...Bubby adores drinking coffee outside, Whether that be on El Paseo, or on the deck of her home, she loves to sip and listen to the wonders of nature...So when we want to hang out, there's no debating what we'll be doing. Once it's time to go, she always sends me home with treats...When I was younger, she used to have a huge bucket of coins and I was allowed one scoop with my hand and whatever I could grab I could take home, I usually had two scoops compared to my older siblings with bigger hands who only got one...Now, she sends us home with food or limoncello...I love my Italian grandmother and I am so proud of her.

– **Emily Solis, Granddaughter**

January

Day 1 — January 1

MANY TIMES GOD saves the best for last. God's word says, "Your latter years will be better than your former years." I've hung onto that scripture throughout my adult life, and I have found that it's absolutely true… Never dread getting older! Old age is a wonderful experience. Wisdom truly increases with every day that passes, and "Gray hair is a sign of wisdom." Not quite sure what happened to my hair because it has never turned gray, but I still feel a lot wiser. Have a blessed year as we all turn one year older.

AS WE BEGIN a new year, let's purpose in our hearts to look to God for everything and remind Him of His promises. He tells us, "Lean not on your own understanding, but acknowledge Him in all your ways, and He will direct your path." Let's start the new year by acknowledging Him first thing every day and getting that path straightened out. Happy New Year.

Day 2   January 2

GOD LOVES ALL of us, but God's favor on us has to do with obedience, and I believe if you have the favor of God on you… you've got it all. The word says that "Jesus grew in favor with God and man." So, this means that we can actually grow in favor with God. We grow in God's favor when we choose to do it God's way, whether we agree or not…

ASK GOD EVERY day that you will show up well for this day and then trust Him for tomorrow. He tells us not to be anxious for anything and that "today has enough troubles of its own, so don't worry about tomorrow." Deal efficiently with the troubles of the day and release the worry to God. And never fret over tomorrow! "Fret not, it will only cause harm."

Day 3   January 3

THE BEST TEACHING is usually 70% things that you already know, and that 70% causes you to grasp the other 30% of fresh teaching. There are times when we can hear something over and over, but "until we have ears to hear," we don't grasp it. A good teaching will lead you to the threshold of your own understanding. Usually, when you finally get it... you already knew 70% of it. Always be open to new things and just be sure they line up with God's word.

HAPPINESS IS WHEN your circumstances are all in order, while joy comes from the blessings of God. Happiness is fleeting, and it comes and goes in your life depending on how things are going, while joy comes from deep within and is not dependent on what is going on around you. That joy is connected to the peace that God gives to His children. "My peace I leave with you, not like the world can give, but only like I can give." So, instead of saying "Happy New Year." I say to you, "Have a joyous New Year."

Day 4   January 4

QUEEN ELIZABETH HAD a line that I loved... She said, "Don't complain, and don't explain... just get on with it!" And even though it's not scripture, I think it fits perfectly with "Forgetting the things that are behind and moving toward the things that are ahead." So, in essence, stop your whining, stop defending yourself, and go do what you know you need to do. "Acknowledge God as you go, and He will direct your steps."

SOMETIMES THINGS GET so broken that they cannot be put back together—things that are just not going to get better. These are the things that we just have to live with... There's no need to whine and complain... we just need to get used to dealing with these sorts of situations. We don't have to ask God why... Sometimes it's the choices of others that cause it, and sometimes it's just the fallen man syndrome—or even our own choices—that have caused it. Remember, there are consequences to every choice. "But whether you abase or whether you abound, praise God in everything." Get over it and get on with it.

Day 5   January 5

FIND THE BALANCE. "God loves a just and balanced weight." This includes every area of life—from the weight on your scales to your spending habits, your friendships, your projects and work, and everything else. And if you budget some time in for God, you will find that your life will automatically balance out. "Seek God and His kingdom first, and everything else will be added."

"I PRAY ABOVE all things that you should prosper and be in good health, just as your soul prospers." Jesus actually said that He prayed for these things above everything else for us... but it has a deeper meaning. The word prosper, as defined in the Bible, means *help along the way*. This includes every area of life and not just money and possessions. Health, defined Biblically, means solid, whole, safe, and sound, as well as physically healthy. Claim this wonderful prayer that Jesus prayed for us... Have a prosperous and healthy New Year.

Day 6   January 6

"WOULD YOU STILL love God even if it looked like you weren't blessed? What if you got sick and lost everything? Would you stand strong and still believe? Job had to experience such life trials... and in the end, he was blessed beyond measure because he never gave up on God through all of the trials. "Though He may slay me, yet will I serve Him." Sometimes God does allow certain things, but it will always "work toward good for those who believe." "Only believe."

IF YOU WILL show up, be teachable, and serve others, your growth and success in life are practically guaranteed. There lies a commitment in showing up, and there lies humility in being teachable and serving others... and these are things that most people buck. But I guarantee you, if you submit your life to these three simple standards, you will find the life that God has planned for you. "I have a good plan for your life—a plan to prosper you and not to harm you."

Day 7   January 7

RIGHTEOUS ANGER IS permissible, and even Jesus got mad. Anger is a very dangerous thing when it is out of order, but righteous anger is not only acceptable—it is necessary to get things done. When you feel righteous anger... step up and do something about it. We are told to be "strong and courageous," and there are times that we need to go in swinging.

EVERYBODY WANTS A new beginning, but with every new beginning comes the death of something. You have to die to self to get a new beginning. Whether you're looking to quit smoking, lose weight, get new friends, or buy a new house—no matter where your new beginning lies, you will have to give something else up! You have to make room for the new, which means you have to get rid of the old. God never tells us to look backward; He only says, "Reach toward those things that are ahead and forget the things that are behind." Let go of the old and receive the new.

Day 8   January 8

KEEP ASKING GOD, and do not be discouraged because your prayers are not immediately answered. Silence is not a "no" with God. "There is a time and a season for everything under the sun." Stand in the presence of God as you wait for the positive answer to your prayer. Many times, God is silent because He's working some things out. Never give up on prayer... and persist.

"GOD'S FAVOR RESTS upon those who urgently seek Him." It is when you truly know that you need God that a mega blessing falls upon you. "In your weakness, God is made strong." Admit your weakness. The world says that Jesus is a crutch... and for once, the world is right. I lean on that crutch every day of my life, and I hope you do too.

Day 9   January 9

WE LIVE IN a fallen world, and we are subject to the issues it causes. It is not God who caused the fallen world, but rather the sins of man. We all need a secret place where we find peace with Jesus— "A peace like only He can give... not like the world gives, but only like Jesus can give." A quiet place where we can separate ourselves... We do not have to be victims of this fallen world when we have a relationship with Jesus. "Draw close to God, and He will draw close to you."

SIMPLIFY TO AMPLIFY. Sometimes we set our goals so lofty that we cannot reach them, and we give up. The old adage that says, *"Keep it simple, stupid,"* has lots of merit. There is nothing wrong with setting lofty goals for the future, but it is extremely important to keep the steps simple. It is much like climbing a ladder—you know you are heading for the top, but for now, you only take the next step. Keeping your mind set on what you can do today to achieve the lofty goal will help simplify the project. "Don't worry about the problems of tomorrow, because today has enough problems of its own."

Day 10   January 10

DO NOT BE offended by the stupidity and insensitivity of people. Keep a humble and hopeful perspective, and do not allow yourself to take offense. Many times, offense is taken when none was even intended, and other times, it was intended... but rise above the insensitivity of man, and God will bless you. "Good sense makes one slow to anger, and it is to his glory to overlook an offense."

GEORGE ORWELLS LAST words were, "You die with the face you deserve," and you know what? He was right... Always remember that what you allow to stay in your head will eventually show up on your face. "Take every thought captive." Do not let negativity and fear sneak into your mind. Your words and thoughts can change your whole life.

Day 11   January 11

WE LIVE IN a culture that believes it is OK to do whatever you believe is right. This will create a chaotic culture. God has laid out rules for mankind that will create a safe, peaceful, happy culture. It does not matter how many people go down a path… Take the path that God has laid out for you, "A holy highway that no evil thing may come upon." "Broad and wide is the path to destruction, and many shall travel it, but narrow and straight is the path to heaven, and few will choose it."

"THIS IS AMAZING. Read it all!!! The word "Believe" is in the Bible 272 times. "Pray" is there 371 times, and "Love" is there 714 times, but the word "Give" is there a whopping 2,162 times!! Wow, if you are not a giver, you are totally blocking your blessings. Did you know that statistically, generous people rarely have mental illnesses of any kind? They usually have more friends and are happier in general. The root word of miserable is "miser." Stingy people will always be miserable!! Bless yourself and others by being a giver. "Give, and it shall be given unto you, pressed down, shaken together, and running over shall men give unto your bosom." I like it!!

Day 12   January 12

"GOD OPPOSES THE proud but gives grace to the humble." If you want more of God's grace in your life... Be humble. One of the key elements of humility is to give other people credit... Even if you think the credit belongs to you! This is a hard one, but it is the epitome of humility. Puffed-up pride may, at a glance, appear handsome... When, in fact, "Pride comes before a fall."

"DO NOT BE afraid, little flock... it gives me pleasure to bless you." I just absolutely love that scripture. When Jesus is your Lord, every day can be characterized by glory and joy. Watch for those little pleasures of blessing that your Father in heaven delights to bestow on you, little flock

Day 13   January 13

GOD KNOWS THOSE who are His. He knows your heart and what you look like... and your possessions have nothing to do with your acceptance by God. People tend to judge you by your clothes, your looks, and your possessions, but God only sees your heart... "We are judged by what's in our heart," not by anything else. God loves you just the way you are.

IT'S NEVER WRONG to do what's right, even if it means putting you at a disadvantage. God is always on the side of right, and He opposes anything that is wrong. And you never want to set yourself up on the wrong side of God. God wins every time. "Trust Him with all your heart and lean not on your own understanding, and He will direct your path."

Day 14 January 14

GOD DOES TEST and examine us, and many times your trials are just a test to find out what is really in your heart. This is why God says to "count it all joy when you go through the fiery trials because it is perfecting you." Trials expose our deficiencies and lack of faith and actually refine us. Be encouraged and learn from your trials. "God is faithful to finish the work He has started in you."

THE BIBLE WILL totally change when taken out of context. I liken it to a complicated puzzle. If you only look at one piece in the box, the impression is completely distorted. And yet, this is how the Bible is often interpreted. The only place in the Bible that you can look at one scripture and have it be pretty much complete is the book of Proverbs. Most of the other scriptures, you must read what is before and after the scripture to get the full meaning. "Study to make yourself approved."

Day 15   January 15

"CONSIDER YOUR WAYS" Does it seem that you live paycheck to paycheck? Is your life a struggle? Are you tending to the things of God? Because life will not go well if you are not tending to the things of God. Your land will be filled with milk and honey when you honor God with your first fruits. He promises "you will not lack any good thing." When you honor God first, you will always have everything you need and more.

YOU WILL BECOME what you repeatedly do. It is said that it takes three weeks to form a solid habit… So, you can imagine when you say or do something over and over that eventually this will become what you are known for and permeate your whole life. Be intentional with words and habits and remember. "Your tongue has the power to speak life and death." Watch your words!

Day 16   January 16

NEVER ALLOW YOURSELF to be content with that which cannot satisfy. The things of the world are so temporal and unsatisfying, and the more you have, the more you want... Only the things of God can give you "the peace that goes beyond understanding, not like the world gives." "But from this day forward I will bless you." Claim this wonderful promise as you make the choice to put God first.

BUSYNESS CAN BLOCK your spiritual life. If you are too busy, you need to prune your life. Learn to say no to frivolity and say yes to the things of God, and sometimes even accepting to do the right thing is wrong if it causes you to race through life. Nothing gets done right when you are always in a hurry. Slow down and smell the roses... and schedule plenty of time for prayer. "You have not because you ask not."

Day 17   January 17

ARE THINGS NOT working in your life? You eat and drink but you never have enough... You earn wages, but it seems you have a bag with holes in it? Until you serve God, you will never be satisfied... You will plant and have very little harvest... Good things will be like an evasive whirlwind. Stop and consider your ways and make adjustments that include God. "God is able to bless you abundantly, so that in all things at all times, having all that you need, with plenty to help others."

"GOD WILL RESTORE the years the canker worms have eaten" If things have been uprooted, destroyed, stolen, or lost, God promises a restoration. Remember that the restoration doesn't always come in the same form as your loss. Oftentimes we get so busy lamenting over what we have lost that we miss the replacement. This is a promise from God, and when he promises something... Believe it and expect it!

Day 18   January 18

DO NOT LOSE your sense of purpose, or life will never be fulfilling. Your life will be a bag full of holes until you fulfill the purpose that God has for you. Your number one purpose is to honor and glorify God, and produce good fruit. If you are not honoring God, you will feel empty. It is so fruitless to live for self rather than for the glory of God. "Seek first the kingdom of God and his righteousness, and all other things will be added."

HARD WORK AND big dreams are a dynamic duo... If you dream big dreams, and you don't put your hand to some action, it's nothing but pie in the sky. But if you're a hard worker and you start taking steps, even if it's baby steps towards your dream... And you keep your hands moving, you're gonna do this... "God blesses the work of your hands."

Day 19 January 19

WHEN WE SUFFER for any reason, we can either curse God and suffer more or we can trust God and grow. Remember that God can redeem and reverse anything that has happened in our life. Even if we feel frightened, or worry, it does not mean we are not trusting God. Oft times the flesh reacts while the spirit remains strong. Be kind to your human frailties… "The flesh is weak, but the spirit is strong" find a specific promise for your situation and quote it out loud and then "only believe"

PHILOSOPHY IS THE fundamental study of human knowledge, especially words. "Beware that you will not be cheated by the words of men…today, mankind has tended to study philosophy more than the Bible and actually attempt to exult it above the Bible. "Those who think themselves wise will become fools" test every truth by the word of God.

Day 20 — January 20

"THOSE WHO EXALT themselves will be humbled and those who humble themselves will be exalted." Be careful when you think you are above others because God has a way of humbling you. "Don't consider yourself more important than you ought" because just about the time you think that you've got it all together... You may find yourself tumbling down. On the other hand, if you truly show humility, God will exalt you.

"BLESSED ARE THE poor in spirit." The reference to the poor in spirit in this scripture is referring to those who know they need God. It is not referring to the financially poor, the weak, the sick, or anyone else who is in great need, either physically, financially, or psychologically. It is referring to those who know that without God they are nothing... That's where a blessing will fall upon mankind. "I can do all things through Christ who strengthens me." And without him... I am nothing!!!

Day 21   January 21

IT IS OFTEN said that you should never talk about religion or politics... And yet these are the two things that are the backbone of America. And these two things are what are used to take over a country. Jesus tells us as Christians to "go into all the world and preach the gospel," in other words... Talk about religion... And politics are directly tied to our faith, so in this person's humble opinion, if you refrain from talking about religion and politics, you are not doing the work that God has called you to do. This does not mean we are to argue about it.

FAITH AND TRUST are not the same thing, faith is based on a specific promise, while trust is believing God no matter what. Trust is the strongest of the two and really the most valuable... trust comes before faith... and "faith is the only thing that pleases God." "Trust is just knowing that no matter what happens in life, God is going to take care of it. You don't need to have any Bible scripture or any proof... You just know that you know, that you know, that God has his hand on you. A truly coveted position to be in.

Day 22   January 22

SOMETIMES THINGS HAPPEN in our life, and things just blow up and everything is out of control… all you can do is trust God to bring things back into his alignment. Trust that God will use your trials to align with what he has planned for you. These trials will "work towards good" and eventually be part of the plan that God has for you. "All things work together for good to he that loves God and is called according to God's purpose for them" … All things!!!!

WHEN JESUS IS your wonderful counselor, you don't just see stars in the sky, you see God's glory. This glory is invisible to those who have not given their heart to this wonderful counselor, but when he has your heart, he abides in you and you see things through his eyes and there is a glory beyond any description. "Call unto me and I will abide in you and you will abide in me."

Day 23   January 23

WE NEVER KNOW when God might be doing something, even when things do not appear to be him at all. He does work in strange ways and we are often tempted to reject things that are actually God doing a work. A way that seems strange might actually be the thumbprint of God. Because "his ways are so different from our ways." We never know how or why God does things the way he does, but we do know the outcome of his miracle hand in our life. "Be strong and courageous" as you journey through the issues of life, trusting that "God will never leave you nor forsake you."

IT IS SAID that God works in mysterious ways and this is so absolutely true… Jesus did some strange things. He spit on people, put mud on their eyes, and put his fingers on people's tongues. All of this and more to bring about healing. Never put God in a box. He might use anything to perform his will. He has even been known to speak through the mouth of a donkey. Stay open and aware as you watch for a word or move from God. "His thoughts are higher than ours and his ways are higher than our ways."

Day 24   January 24

DON'T WASTE YOUR suffering, let it strengthen you. We all have times of suffering and God can use your suffering to teach you many things. "Suffering produces perseverance, and perseverance produces perfection and strength." Do everything you know to do to fix things and "after you've done everything you know to do, stand and believe." Do not wait on God until you have done everything you know to do! And if while you're waiting, you find something else you can do… Do it!

THERE ARE THOSE who once they start doing good, they think they don't need God anymore, and they walk away… In this case, God's blessings can be more dangerous than his burdens. No matter where you find yourself, "Draw close to God and he will draw close to you." Do not just seek God when you're in trouble, stay close to him all the time and you won't be as likely to get in trouble…

Day 25   January 25

IF A PERSON does not use their God-given talents for God… Eventually, they will use it for the enemy. One way or another your talents will be used… Make a choice today that all of your gifts and talents are going to be dedicated to God. If you do not dedicate your talents to God… Eventually you will self-destruct. "Whatever you do, do it all for the glory of God."

TREASURE GOD'S WORD…HANG on to his word as if it were gold, because it is. Take God's word for yourself and tuck it away in your heart and your head, and in so doing, it will eventually come out of your mouth. "Out of the abundance of the heart, the mouth speaks." And when the mouth speaks, the power of life and death is in the tongue, so when it begins to come out of your mouth…your life becomes solidly established.

Day 26   January 26

GEORGE WASHINGTON ONCE said: "Right makes might." In other words, when you do things right, you will have strength in your life. Right living brings about a power like nothing else. Always do what you know to be right and as you dispense righteousness and integrity in your life, it will always come back to you, "Pressed down, shaken together and running over…in whatever measure you give, it will be given unto you."

YOU ARE GOING to be tested in life, and when you pass the test, blessings will always follow. We all have issues and need God, so don't let your flesh mess with your mind, because God does hear your cry and he does care…Trials and troubles will always befall believers but remember that "God takes pleasure in the prosperity of his children," and prosperity is not only monetary, it is in every area of your life. Be encouraged.

Day 27 — January 27

MARGARET THATCHER ONCE said, "Compromisers are those who stand in the middle of the road and hope not to get hit by a car," and she is absolutely right... God says, "If you are lukewarm, he will spew you out of his mouth." "Let your yea be yea and your nay be nay." Be bold and respectful but stand up for what you believe in and know to be true.

GOD IS UNCHANGING. Hold tight to his unchanging hand as you travel this journey we call life. The world and all it stands for is crumbling at an alarming rate and the road they travel is not only broad and easy to flow along with, but it is destructive beyond words these days. Stay on that straight, narrow path that few will travel...that path that is "a holy highway, one which no evil thing may come upon," and one that is filled with beautiful treasures at every turn.

Day 28 January 28

ADVERSE CIRCUMSTANCES ARE normal in the fallen world... But thank God that "Jesus has overcome the world." Those who put their hope in him will always be able to not only overcome these adverse circumstances, but they will actually find treasures in the wake of them, and have them work towards good... I pray that Jesus is your Lord so you can claim all these wonderful promises that belong to those who call him Lord.

A FRUITFUL LIFE will be a life worth living, and life will always be a happy joyous life. Keep yourself busy all the days of your life. Did you know that the word retirement isn't even in the Bible, it actually says, "They will still bear fruit in old age, they will stay fresh and green." Much like the date trees, whose fruit gets sweeter, the older the tree gets. I don't know about you, but I plan on bearing sweet fruit all the days of my life, and I definitely want to stay fresh and green. Thank you, Jesus.

Day 29   January 29

ALWAYS BE FAITHFUL with the little things, because every worthy outcome always starts small! The huge, important, successful things in life are always a compilation of many small, seemingly insignificant issues on their own, but together they compile the grandiose. "Be faithful with a little, and you will become ruler over much."

PROVERBS SAYS "WHERE there is strife, there is pride, but wisdom is found in those who take advice." It is so difficult to deal with people who will not own their own mistakes. They give you a reason why you are wrong and they are right. Or they make an excuse for why they did it... The wise man hears rebuke or constructive criticism and makes the needed changes, while the fool prattles on about why he did it and suffers the consequences.

Day 30 — January 30

WHEN DIVISION HAPPENS, discouragement will prevail and projects will be thwarted. Agreement is so powerful: "Two are better than one because we have a good reward for our work." Discouragement is one of the worst enemies of mankind. Stir yourself and each other up. Do not allow discouragement and division to take you down.

IF YOU HAVE a need, you have to ask God for it. "You have not because you ask not." People amaze me who say things like, *my needs are too small... God has enough to do* as if he can't do it all! Remember, our God is omnipotent, nothing is too small or too big for him. If it matters to you, it matters to God. And as long as your request is within his promises for you, "you shall have whatever you ask."

Day 31

January 31

THE WORD "BELIEVE" is in the Bible 272 times. "Pray" is there 371 times, and "Love" is there 714 times, but the word "Give" appears a whopping 2,162 times! Wow, if you are not a giver, you are totally blocking your blessings. Did you know that, statistically, generous people rarely have mental illnesses of any kind? They usually have more friends and are happier in general. The root word of miserable is "miser." Stingy people will always be miserable! Bless yourself and others by being a giver. "Give and it shall be given unto you, pressed down, shaken together, and running over shall men give unto your bosom." I like it!

"EVERY PLACE ON which the sole of your foot treads shall be yours." This is actually a promise from the Old Testament, and I think it's high time we take God's word for what it says. If you live in an area, claim it, speak blessings over it, take care of it, and defend it. Even if you don't legally own something, God has given you the blessing in the spirit realm. Leave any place you find yourself better than you found it.

PROVERBS 4:7 SAYS, "The beginning of wisdom is this: Get wisdom and whatever you get, get insight." Seeking Godly wisdom through all of life's twist and turns is challenging. Where and how does one get wisdom? Don't worry Bubby will unravel this mystery with her devotions. But I suggest reading them in private because who knows you might be laughing; you might be crying, and you may realize you were the one with the bad attitude earlier(oops). But no matter what you will conclude with a greater understanding of God's wisdom.

– **Audrey Solis Granddaughter**

MY BUBBY IS the picture of wisdom, fearlessness, and rarity…Throughout my life she has been my blueprint of what it means to work hard, have a giving spirit, and trust that God's will always provide. Carrying the family middle name, Gladys—passed down from her mother to her and now to me—is a blessing and an honor.

– **Gracie Gladys Solis, Granddaughter**

 February

Day 32 — February 1

WHEN WE WALK in humility, we receive God's grace and mercy, but when we walk in arrogance and pride, we bring a curse on ourselves. If we refuse to humble ourselves before God, we will be exposed, and God himself will humble us. "God resists the proud but gives grace to the humble," and there's nothing sweeter than the grace of God in our life.

FORGIVENESS IS THE responsibility of the victim—the one who has been hurt. Love and forgiveness cannot, nor should, be earned. If someone has done you harm, it is up to you to forgive them. They have their own issues, and you cannot worry about how they respond or what they do. It is up to you to forgive them! "Forgive others so that God will forgive you." And remember, "If you hold aught against any man when you stand praying, God does not hear your prayers." That should shake you to the core. Forgive!

Day 33　　　　　　　　　　February 2

WHEN I READ this writing, my eyes welled up with tears. Many may not grasp its profound impact, but to truly understand, one must know the Father well. I only wish I had written it.

When Moses asked God His name, He answered with YHWH, which, when spoken in its original Hebrew form, sounds like breathing—YH (inhale), WH (exhale). A baby's first cry and a person's last breath both speak His name. Even an atheist, unknowingly, acknowledges Him with every breath.

In sadness, we sigh His name. In joy, our lungs feel full. In fear, we hold our breath, then inhale to calm ourselves. Before difficult tasks, we take deep breaths for courage. Every breath is an act of praise—even in hardship.

God chose a name we cannot help but speak every moment we are alive. Waking, sleeping, breathing—His name is always on our lips.

OUR WORDS HAVE the power to impact others for a lifetime. They can be apologized for and forgiven, but once they are out there, they cannot be retrieved. Words can destroy a relationship and a life. Be intentional with your words, especially with young people. You can make or break a young person with what you tell them about themselves. "The power of life and death is in the tongue." Use this powerful weapon to bless and not curse yourself and others.

Day 34 — February 3

GOD'S PROMISES HAVE never failed!! "He is not a man that He should lie... has He not said it, and will He not do it?" Find these promises and hang on to them. Everything of God will experience a purging and a shaking and will be put through the test... but stand strong and do not waver. God's promises are forever, and what cannot be shaken is what will remain in the end."

YOU HAVE TO have a goal... If you don't have a goal, how can you hit your target? It would be like trying to shoot a bow and arrow at a target when it's not there. Write it down, "Acknowledge God, and He will make your path straight." Make a plan and then put action to it as you climb the ladder one step at a time. Whatever your goal is, take the first step towards it, even if it is a baby step. Stop talking and dreaming and put some action to your dream.

Day 35 — February 4

THERE IS NO greater promise in the Bible than "I am with you." What an amazing consideration... He is always with us, even in the mud and scum of life. He promises to "never leave us or forsake us." Always remember that. You have God's promise for that. Fear not... God is with you.

SOMETIMES WE NEED to deviate from our routine, especially if we sense some sort of breakdown. Sometimes we can get so caught up in doing the exact same thing at the exact same time that we become stagnant and bored. Change can be so refreshing, and it has been proven by many studies that those who keep the mind active and refreshed will stay younger. "Forget the things that are behind and move towards the things that are ahead."

Day 36 — February 5

IF YOU HAVE failures in your life that you regret, as we all do... Do not disqualify yourself from serving God. Give your failures over to God and trust Him to "finish the work He has started in you." We all have regrets, but guilt will imprison you in your past. God never uses guilt to punish you. Live your life with confidence, and remember, if you have asked God for forgiveness, "He doesn't even remember your sin anymore." Why should you remember it?

YOUR MIND IS a magnet... What you focus on is what will manifest itself in your life. If you are spending your time focusing on the ugly things in this world, you are going to draw that to yourself. There are plenty of good things to focus on. Remember that God tells us to "think on the things that are lovely, beautiful, noble, praiseworthy, and good..." He tells us that for a reason, and we need to take Him at His word.

Day 37 — February 6

DO NOT COMPARE yourself one to the other because it will either cause you to feel inferior or prideful. Comparison is never productive and will almost always bring about envy and jealousy... and "where there is envy and jealousy, there is also every other evil working." Do the best you can with what you have been given, and you will achieve your own personal greatness.

BE COMFORTABLE BEING uncomfortable because it is perfecting you, and "in your weakness, God is made strong." Your life may not go as planned, you may not win the race or cross that coveted finish line that you had planned, but I assure you that if you keep getting back up again when you fall and stay in the race, you will have a good finish. "Run your race as if to win."

Day 38 — February 7

"A GOOD MAN" brings forth good with the good that is stored up within him. Be careful what you see and hear because that is what you will store up, and it will eventually manifest into reality. Do good to others, even in simple ways, and although we can't help everyone, we can positively affect those who come within our sphere of influence. And remember… "When you put perfume on someone, you will get some of it on yourself."

OUR FAITH AND hope should be in God, not in the world, your bank account, who is in the White House, or even your family or loved ones. All of these things can and will let you down. But "God is the same yesterday, today, and tomorrow," and "He will never leave you or forsake you."

Day 39   February 8

GOD ONLY GIVES us as much as He knows we can manage. According to the size of our assignment and the season that we are in is how God will provide. Be willing to accept your own personal provision. God will always give you enough. And I still believe the best way to get blessed is by the work of your own hands. "God blesses the work of your hands."

WHEN IT LOOKS like everything has gone amok and it looks like evil has won... always remember that good will always win in the end. Choose what you know to be right because this keeps God on your side, and stay encouraged... "There may be tears at night, but joy will come in the morning." Believe for the miraculous and trust God.

Day 40 — February 9

THERE ARE FOUR different ways that God may use to bless you. One way is through the hand of man, as He gives you favor and causes men to be generous toward you. The second way is through His own hand as He supernaturally provides miraculous-type provisions. The third way is our own hand, as He promises to "bless the work of our hands." And fourth, He even promises to "set a table before us in the presence of our enemies," so He even uses our enemies to bless us. But regardless of how God blesses you, remember, it is always from Him, no matter how He gets it to you.

DREAMS WILL NOT do you any good unless you experience movement into the natural. Dreams have to materialize, or they are worthless. "The work of your hands" is the key to the manifestation of dreams. God promises to "bless the work of the hands," even if you're a scoundrel... this is a principle that works for both the saved and the unsaved... so keep your hands moving.

Day 41 — February 10

"AND THOUGH YOUR beginnings were small, your latter days will be great." I love this scripture, and I have walked it out in my own life. When we choose to trust God, He will take us to our own personal mountaintop. Everyone's mountaintop is different, but yours belongs only to you, and when you trust God and travel your journey with integrity, you will reach your own personal plateau, wherein lies the true peace of God.

IT TAKES ONE idiot to complain, and it takes two idiots to make an argument out of it. Don't allow yourself to get into petty arguments with people who oppose your opinion. Socrates once said, "I can't teach anybody anything, I can only make them think." A kind, gentle response to an opposing opinion might cause someone to think about your side of things. "A gentle answer turns away wrath."

Day 42 — February 11

HARD TIMES CREATE strong men, strong men create good times, good times create weak men, and weak men create hard times, and that, my friends, is the circle of life. Be one of those people who get stronger because of hardships. God tells us "to count it all joy when we go through fiery trials because it is perfecting us." Learn what you're supposed to learn as you go through the trials and create good times.

OUR LIFE IS limited by our flesh, our ability, our education, finances, circumstances— all sorts of things limit what we are able to do on our own... But always remember that God does not have any limitations. "What is impossible with man is possible with God." A simple "Help me, Lord" is a powerhouse prayer that can accomplish more than you could ever imagine. "I can do all things through Christ who strengthens me."

Day 43　　　　　　　　　　　February 12

FEAR OF GOD is drastically different than any other fear. Fear of the Lord is a source of great blessing... This fear is not like a negative dread, but rather it provides a holy awe that brings a holy reverence of respect and amazement, and along with this comes every blessing known to mankind. There are 39 promises attached to the fear of the Lord, and one of them is a promise of a gift of protection as "the angels encamp around those who fear Him," and "they will never lack any good thing." I love these promises, and I claim them for myself.

"YOU WILL MAKE known to me the way of life; in Your presence is fullness of joy, in Your right hand there are pleasures forever." I don't know about you, but this scripture absolutely delights me, and I plan on staying in His presence all the days of my life, reveling in the fullness of joy and expecting Him to show me great and mighty things. What a comfort!

Day 44   February 13

WHEN WE RESPOND to the awesomeness of God, it encompasses the fear of God. He is able to do absolutely anything He chooses to do, and He should be loved, respected, and yes, feared. Never, never treat Jesus or God flippantly! "The fear of the Lord is the beginning of wisdom." Are you sure you're showing God the fear and reverence that He deserves and requires of us? The blessings of God will never fall on those who do not fear Him.

YOU DO NOT need to go to anyone else to have them pray for you, because all of us have been given the power to go directly to God. A go-between is not necessary, even though it is wonderful to come into agreement with a like-minded person in prayer. Take your needs directly to God and communicate with Him just as if He's in the room with you. "The effectual fervent prayers of a righteous man avail much."

Day 45 — February 14

MARTIN LUTHER KING once said, "I have decided to stick with love because hate is too great of a burden to contain," and I think today, on Valentine's Day, it is a perfect time to remember that love is what makes the world go round. It is what makes life joyous and happy, it is the heart of mankind, and it certainly is the heart of God. Have a blessed Valentine's Day as you remember your loved ones.

"WHAT IS LOVE?" Love is the result of keeping covenant with God, and God commands the man to love his wife, but He never once commands a wife to love her husband. Wives are told to "honor your husband," and if you commit to love, your love will grow. Love is a verb; it is movement, not just a feeling. You *do* love rather than just feel love. Guide and direct your love towards your mate by "considering them more important than yourself." Love is a commitment to give yourself to another. Adore is a combination of love, respect, and honor, and I personally love the word "cherish." When you are cherished, you are truly loved. Happy Valentine's Day. Be especially sweet to those you love today.

Day 46   February 15

WE SHOULD MAKE plans for the future but remember to live in the now... Plans are only a potential, while the now is very real. Flow with the changes in life that you have no control over and make the best of every situation. Life is filled with ups and downs, ins and outs, and many bumpy roads... Make the best out of your life journey and enjoy the moment as you trust God to "direct your steps."

AS A CHRISTIAN, we don't just see the problem, but we see God's glory in everything. We know that "nothing is impossible with God," so we can trade fear and doubt for joy. And we also know that "all things work together for good to those that love God." So this removes all fear and concern about the future. Such an amazing promise. There are over 6,000 promises in the Bible... Find them and remind yourself and God what they say.

Day 47　　　　　　　　　　February 16

PARTING WORDS!!! DO you realize that every time you leave someone or talk to them, it could be the last time you ever see them or are able to share something with them? Be intentional when you bid someone farewell, even if you're just talking to someone that you speak with daily. "The power of life and death is in your tongue." Always speak life into your relationships. Be sweet. Life is short.

"YOU WILL MAKE" known to me the way of life." This is a wonderful promise. God will show you things you do not know when you look to Him and "acknowledge Him in all your ways." He will lead you along paths that are safe as He warns and guides you through your day. A simple prayer of "Guide me, Lord" every morning to start your day is a powerful prayer.

Day 48   February 17

WHEN YOU CHOOSE to leave the path of God, you are choosing the evil that is everywhere... You are choosing to walk in the reign of evil. God says there is a path that is like a "holy highway that no evil thing may come upon." When you choose to follow the principles that God has laid out for our good, you're choosing to walk on that holy highway.

FAITH IS BELIEVING without seeing... And God says, "Blessed are those who have never seen and yet still believe." When we choose to "walk by faith and not by sight," we are choosing God's favor and His blessing upon us. "Without faith, it is impossible to please God." I love the short scripture that says, "Only believe."

Day 49   February 18

WHEN YOU CHOOSE to tithe... This is giving 10% of all of your income... God says that "He will rebuke the devourer for your sake." Tithing is one of the things that brings enormous blessings into your life. For me, it is like a kindergarten lesson because it is so simple, and yet it is one of the hardest things to get people to do. But if you want to get blessed... Just do it! It works! It is the only place in the Bible that God tells you to "try Him."

GOD'S WORD WILL always prosper and bring peace to those who hear it and receive it. I did not choose to hear or receive God's word until I was 41 years old... And what a difference it has made in my life. I cannot even imagine being in this dark world without the comfort and peace that I get from knowing that my Father in heaven has His hand on me and that I am "walking on a holy highway that no evil thing may come upon." Thank you, Jesus.

Day 50 — February 19

THE FEAR OF the Lord is not just an Old Testament thing. God is huge, He is omnipotent, and yes, He is our Father, but "the fear of the Lord" should never be forgotten. Never think that God will not or cannot decide to zap all of us. Love and respect are synonymous. "The angels of the Lord encamp around those who fear Him." "The fear of the Lord is the beginning of wisdom." "There will always be an abundance for those who fear Him."

REMEMBER TO KEEP your hands moving! "God blesses the work of your hands." You can't sit around waiting for God... Get moving! I see way too many Christians who are not blessed financially, and I will guarantee you, it is the work of your hands or the words of your mouth that are blocking your progress. God says that "He wishes above all things that we would prosper and be in good health." Financial prosperity is directly connected to your mouth and the work of your hands... Keep your hands moving and watch your mouth.

Day 51 — February 20

WHEN IT SEEMS you are just stranded and life is passing you by... See an opportunity while you are down or feel left out... This could prove to be a unique chance to receive a miracle. "In our weakness, God is made strong." Spend this time to draw closer to God... This is a perfect opportunity to explore a deeper relationship with Him. When I take the time to really just dump everything out before God, I always feel so much better. Try it.

IF YOU GIVE more than just money, if you give mercy, love, understanding, and compassion, as well as money and stuff, God will open the windows of heaven, and your life will be overflowing with blessings. It is truly "more blessed to give than to receive." Share something today, and watch your own spirits lift.

Day 52   February 21

WE ARE NOT required to follow an evil ruler. Even though we are told that "every authority is established by God," He establishes them, and they have an obligation to stay within the perimeters of their Godly appointing. When they step out of those perimeters, we are no longer required to follow their rules. It is likened to a father who is given the authority by God to be the head of a house, and he tells his children to rob a bank. We are not to submit to evil authorities! It is our duty to expose them. "Vengeance belongs to God," and He will remove them in His timing.

WE WILL ALWAYS go through trials—that is just part of life—but clean things up as best you can as you go along and never give up. If something doesn't work, pick up and move on. Your failures do not define you, and because you failed once, you actually have a better chance of making it next time because, hopefully, you have learned from your mistakes. "Acknowledge God in all your ways, and He will direct your path."

Day 53   February 22

YOUR ACTIONS WILL reveal your faith… The way you act can tell where you really stand. "Faith without works is dead." While words are important, if they do not have action behind them, they are just empty words. Your faith can heal you; be demonstrative about your faith. Words coupled with your actions can move mountains.

PRIDE, PAIN AND pleasure are the three stumbling blocks for mankind to deny or disown God. Do not let the wounds of life, destructive pride, or the temporal pleasures of this world block the greatest gift of all… Jesus. "Pride comes before a fall," and God is actually the answer to your pain. The pleasure of this life is just temporary, while His joy lasts forevermore. Pride, pain, and pleasure over Jesus??? NOT!

Day 54 — February 23

GOD USES ALL sorts of things and people to speak to you and show you things. God even spoke to the prophet Balaam through the mouth of a jackass. This was an extreme example of how God can use absolutely anything to get His point across. "If you go the wrong way... To the right or the left... You'll hear a voice behind you saying, 'This is the way you should go.'" Always be expectant to hear God.

YOUR KINDNESS IS never wasted; it will produce a far greater reward than you could ever expect or imagine. The law of sowing and reaping is a given and cannot be denied. Giving does not decrease, but rather, it increases. "Whatever you give will be given back to you, pressed down, shaken together, and running over." Give of yourself, your stuff, and your money, and watch the increase. Whatever your needs are, give in that area.

Day 55 February 24

LIFE ITSELF WILL challenge your faith. There is always something going on in life that will cause you to question God and His promises. Make an intentional decision that no matter what you see with your eyes, things will get better! The size of your faith does not matter; it is what you put your faith in that matters. "Faith the size of a mustard seed can move a mountain." Natural limitations do not affect God. "With man, some things are impossible, but with God, all things are possible."

PAINS WILL COME and go over a lifetime, but those seasons of pain have built your character. "Count it all joy when you go through fiery trials because it is perfecting you." None of us will escape the pain of life... But as you travel through the trials, remind yourself that "this too shall pass" and "though there may be tears at night, there will be joy in the morning." Life is an exciting journey... Enjoy the ride.

Day 56

February 25

WE ARE LIVING in troubled times, and God calls us to remember His word. With over 6,000 promises given to His people, many of us have taken for granted the blessings we enjoy and have not committed these assurances to heart. Psalm 91, in particular, is filled with powerful promises of protection for those who trust in Him: *"If you say, 'The Lord is my refuge,' and you make the Most High your dwelling, no harm will overtake you... He will command His angels concerning you to guard you in all your ways."* Now more than ever, we should hold on to these scriptures. I encourage you to read and memorize Psalm 91, as its promises may be exactly what we need.

IF WE ENDURE with Christ, we will reign with Him. There is so much fear in the world, but to be brave and endure is to always do the right thing, even when we are afraid. Sheer determination to serve God, no matter the circumstances. I don't know about you, but I want to reign with my Jesus. We endure hardships for Him and live our life accordingly.

Day 57   February 26

FEAR CAN PARALYZE you to the point that you cannot even function, and the only fear that can destroy all other fears is the fear of God. If we do not know the fear of God, all other doors of fear will be open. "Let all the earth fear and stand in awe of God Almighty." "Do not fear what the world fears." Instead, be consumed with the fear of the Lord. "Perfect love casts out all fear."

WE WILL ALWAYS fail if we do not try. There is nothing more pitiful than to see a talented person not attempt to do something for fear of failure… Failure is not the big deal; it is rather apathy that is the big deal—a lack of enthusiasm or concern. Always be willing to give it a shot… Nothing ventured, nothing gained. And remember, if you "acknowledge God in all your ways, He will make your path straight," and even if you fail… "It will work towards good." You can't lose with God on your side.

Day 58   February 27

"THERE WILL ALWAYS be an abundance for those who fear God." This is a promise for a successful life. Be sure that you understand exactly what the fear of the Lord is… and remember, it is not like any other fear… it is a unique combination of agape love, and an intense respect. And when you truly get to that place with God… You will always have an abundance of everything.

SEXUAL PERVERSION, CONFUSION, and addiction are leading men astray. We need to hold tight to the things of God, "When the enemy comes in like a flood, the Lord will raise up a standard against it." There is a flood of filthiness and confusion that is swirling around in our world, and it is sucking people under, as it is flung out there by TV, internet, news media, and even teachers and parents. Stay close to God and "you will only see the reward of the wicked with your eyes, but it will not come near you."

Day 59   February 28

"GROW NOT WEARY of well-doing, because in due season you shall have your reward." Sometimes it is so hard to stand strong when you've waited so long for something... But most times, just before the reward is due, you will feel the most tired... Refuse to give up as you wait for God to deliver your reward, and do not waver. "He who wavers gets nothing from God."

"WHERE SIN BOUNDS, much more so does grace." As we look around, it is difficult to not see sin... it is everywhere. But we need to comfort ourselves with this verse. Sin will always eventually manifest itself in the natural, so obviously, we can see the ugliness around us... while the grace of God is more of a spiritual thing, so it is like the air that flows through and around everything and cannot be seen as it gives life and actually increases its power where there is sin. Puff yourself up and don't be discouraged because just as sin is abounding... Much more so is grace. Hallelujah.

Day 60 — February 29

THERE ARE TIMES in life when a problem has prevailed for a period of time, and we just don't know what to do about it... In cases like this, the best thing is to stand back, trust God, and let some more time pass... In time, "this too shall pass." Stop spinning your wheels and wasting energy on things that you cannot change. "Fret not, it will only cause harm."

"FOR YOU BLESS the righteous, O Lord; You cover him with favor as with a shield." When we choose to honor God and delight Him in our ways, He chooses to favor us with His blessings. There is no greater gift than having God's favor on your life. It is a shield of protection and brings "a peace that goes beyond understanding." I pray that God's favor is on your life.

FOREVER GRATEFUL FOR my Bubby. Everything she's taught me, everything she is, she's a light in my life. Coffee talks early morning overlooking her gorgeous views from her quaint little home will be something I'll cherish forever. Thank you, Bubby, for being unapologetically you.

– Nicole Solis, Granddaughter.

 # March

Day 61   March 1

HAVE A PRIVATE prayer time with God. When you are alone with God, there is no one to discourage or condemn you. It is a time when you will be built up. Sometimes I share things with God that are so intimate, and it feels so good when you turn these troubling thoughts over to Him. Nothing is too small or irrelevant for God. He hears every whispered prayer, and "you have not because you ask not."

IF YOU ARE lacking in doing what you know is your own personal duty, you have no right to ask God for anything. Pay watchful attention to what is your unique duty and be sure you are doing it. This is no time to say that you do not want to get involved. There is a fire burning in our country that will eventually burn to everyone's back door. Do your duty to protect your family, your state, and your country. "Occupy till I come."

Day 62   March 2

"ALL OF THESE blessings shall come upon you and overtake you, because you obey the voice of the Lord your God." Always be willing to do what God asks you to do. You usually know when it is God, because it's something that you would not have thought of, or it might even be something that is completely out of your wheelhouse... If it's pure, and it's peaceful, it's probably God.

BEWARE OF GUILT and shame. Shame says you are doomed to failure, while guilt puts a load on you that hinders success. Shame and guilt are not the same. Guilt is for the person who commits the offense, while shame is usually the result that is carried by association. A Christian should never carry shame or guilt! They are actually a lack of faith and are technically saying that what Jesus did on the cross was not enough... Receive the forgiveness and move forward with a clean slate. "Forgetting those things that are behind and reaching toward those things that are ahead."

Day 63 — March 3

IN THE END, we usually only regret the chances we never took. God has given us a beautiful world to enjoy and subdue... He tells us to "occupy until He comes." I believe that occupation includes the enjoyment and the tending of the earth and all its beauty. Men have destroyed much that God created... But there's still plenty of stuff out there to enjoy... Go for it!

"THE LORD MAKES firm the steps of the one who delights in Him; though he may stumble, he will not fall." What an amazing promise! Always remember that God is guiding your steps if you are seeking Him. Trust Him! He has a plan, and it's a good plan... Never waver about God. He knows where you're going, and though the journey may be long and tedious, and even filled with some potholes, you will get where He has you going if you grow not weary.

Day 64 — March 4

FAITH IN JESUS will radically change your life… It will inspire you and change you forever… It seems like just a simple, ordinary decision, but it is the most incredible, important decision you will ever make. It is your ticket to heaven! It is not your good works that will get you to heaven… "It is by grace you are saved and not by works." Being a good ole boy will not get you to heaven… "You must believe in your heart and confess with your mouth that Jesus is Lord to be saved."

THE DAY OF neutrality will soon be gone. The currents of the filthy flood and the currents of God's flood are so strong that we are unable to stand in the middle. There will soon not be any gray area. Many have chosen to be apathetic in a very troubled time, and this, in itself, is a choice. Which side will you choose? "As for me and my house, we choose the Lord."

Day 65   March 5

WHEN YOU PICK up your cross and follow Jesus, it changes everything... You will suddenly find yourself looking to goodness, joy, and peace. The very fabric of your being will totally change... You will find yourself looking to the light. It will transform you and your family, and your life will be filled with a new joyous light. "Taste and see that the Lord is good."

LEARN TO BE fruitful where God has planted you. If there is no provision where you are, maybe it is time to move on. It is wonderful to be stable and persistent, and persistence works most of the time, but there does come a time when you just need to move on. "God promises to direct the steps of the righteous." Keep your eyes open for God's direction... He will open and close the doors... Be willing to take the steps

Day 66 — March 6

WANT A BETTER life? Serve God by serving other people... He also rewards integrity and faithfulness... Doing the right thing brings rewards... God rewards a Godly influence and doing good to the unlovely... You are also rewarded for how you do your work and for giving of your resources... Everything matters... "God rewards those who diligently seek Him." "God is not unjust to forget your labor of love."

PRAYER WILL ALWAYS strike the winning blow, and then the results will be awarded. You will find that you can do so much more after you have prayed... You will feel stronger, and doors will open for you. And if you have really prayed from your heart, you will find that the burden you may have felt for your prayer subject has lifted. Be a prayer warrior, and God will see that your prayers are answered. "The effectual fervent prayers of a righteous man avails much."

DAY 67   March 7

I FOUND A verse in Chronicles that says, "We do not know what to do, but our eyes are on you." As I read that this morning, I realized that is where we are in our country. We feel powerless against the evil that has come against us in America, the land that God has given us... But I was so encouraged when I read that line, and I give it to you this morning to clutch to your breast... "We don't know what to do, but our eyes are on You."

USE YOUR GROWTH, knowledge, power, and strength that God gifts you with to serve others. This is the whole of what God wants from you. "Those who are to become great in the kingdom of God must first become servants to all." And remember... "If you oppress the poor, you are insulting their Maker." Be kind to everyone, even the unlovable.

Day 68 March 8

"GOD WILL ALWAYS multiply any seed you sow." A seed sown is not always a literal seed... It can be anything good that you put out into the world... And God will always give it back to you, "pressed down, shaken together, and running over." While on the other hand, you can put out bad stuff, and it will produce a like harvest as well... A tomato seed will not produce a harvest of carrots... And the same thing goes with your actions... They are literal seeds that will produce in like kind.

THERE IS A continuous spiritual warfare as well as physical. Just because we can't see something does not mean it isn't there. The spiritual world is very real, and many of us stumble over the effects of it. But remember that God lives in the spiritual realm, and if you keep your eyes on Him, He will guide your steps and protect you from the ravages of the unseen world. "A holy highway will be there, a place where God's ransomed shall walk, and there shall be no evil thing upon their path."

Day 69 — March 9

"YOU ARE ONLY as sick as your secrets." When you choose to stuff things away or sweep them under a rug, you are choosing to bloat yourself with all sorts of problems, including mental and physical illnesses. The Catholics have it right when it comes to confession, and you can do the same thing with a trusted friend. The Word tells us to "confess your sins, one to the other, that you might be healed." No secrets!!!

THE DIRECTION WHERE people are heading is way more important than where they are. I think many of us can look back on our lives and see times when people would have looked at us and wondered where the heck we were going... And yet, we ended up right where we were supposed to be. Thank you, Lord, that you are "faithful to finish the work you have started."

Day 70   March 10

EVERYTHING MATTERS. EVERY single thing we do or say has a consequence. There are rewards for both the good and the bad, and sometimes it seems that people are getting away with things, but there will always be recompense. The day will come that God's vengeance will fall on the unrighteous, and rewards will be paid to the righteous. "Vengeance is mine, says the Lord." And most times, that vengeance will be paid by the natural justice that has been established by God on the earth.

IF YOU HAD only one chance to say something to just one person, who would you say it to, and what would you say? The apostle Paul had such an opportunity with Timothy, and his final words were, "If we are faithless, God will remain faithful." I would tell everyone to "serve God with all your heart because everything else is chasing the wind." What would be your final words?

Day 71 — March 11

WHEN YOU FEAR God, your children will be blessed. "This is the heritage of the righteous, and it goes down even to the 10th generation." "The children of the righteous will defeat evil." Just imagine the gift you're giving your offspring when you serve God... Live your life in fear of the Lord... Not like you fear the boogeyman, but with an enormous reverence and awe. Serve Him in sincerity and in truth... This guarantees a blessing on your offspring.

"I WILL INSTRUCT you and teach you in the way you should go; I will guide you with My eye." This is one of over 6,000 promises in the Bible, and they are so important! Find these treasures... Call them out... And claim them for yourself. Just because treasures are there does not mean they are activated. They must be found and claimed just as any earthly treasure must be treated. "Study to make yourself approved."

Day 72 — March 12

"BE ANGRY, BUT do not sin." Anger is part of life, and many things throughout our day can cause us to jump into anger. But the main thing is, "Do not let the sun go down on your wrath." There are definitely things in life that cause what we call "righteous anger." But to allow this anger to continue for any length of time becomes a sin and a detriment to our health and well-being. "Forgive others so God will forgive you."

EVIL CANNOT LAUGH... They can be maniacal with an evil laughter, but they cannot laugh with a joyous laugh. I believe that laughter, like light, will stave off evil. "A merry heart does good like a medicine." There is nothing better than a good old belly laugh. Just as families that pray together will stay together... I will also add, friends that laugh together will be lifelong friends. Be silly... See the humor in life.

Day 73 — March 13

"A FAITHFUL MAN will abound in blessings." It always pays off to be faithful... God loves a faithful person, and we all long to hear that coveted phrase when we make it to heaven, that says, "Well done, good and faithful servant." If you say you're going to do something... Do it! "Woe to him that makes a vow that he does not keep."

WORDS CHANGE THE world. Watch what you say. Your words are so powerful. Words can build you up or tear you down. God literally formed and transformed the earth with words. Your world around you can change with your words. Gentle, positive words will soften the soil of the heart. Avoid words that destroy. "The power of life and death is in your words."

Day 74   March 14

WORRIES KEPT IN the darkness will grow, but they shrink in the light. "Walk by the light of day, because in the darkness, we stumble." Always be verbal about things that are tormenting you… Share with a trusted friend. Darkness cannot be where there is light. So put light on everything that is ugly in your mind. Be transparent as you share the testimony of your life with others, because "the blood of the Lamb, and the word of your testimony overcomes the enemy." This is the only place in the Bible that anything is compared to the power of the blood of the Lamb… Your testimony! Share it!

GOD USES ORDINARY people to do extraordinary things. Most of the people in the Bible that He used to do great things were not only ordinary, sometimes they were even substandard people… Those that you thought could never be great… Moses stuttered… David was kind of puny… Paul was an unbeliever and killed Christians… And on and on… So don't think that God can't use you. "God has a good plan for your life, a plan to prosper you, and not to harm you."

Day 75   March 15

CARRYING YOUR CROSS means death to your flesh by giving up the comforts of the flesh and living your life to honor and serve God... Our culture wears and displays beautiful crosses, but the truth is that a cross represents suffering and should be a reminder of the suffering that Jesus endured for our freedom... When we choose to pick up our cross and carry it along with Jesus, we are choosing to always do what is right, even if it brings persecution... "If anyone wants to follow after me, he must take up his cross and deny his flesh."

"A BRUISED REED God will not break." God will always be gentle with those who are troubled, and we should also be gentle with those who are struggling with life. It can be so easy to judge people, and I know I am guilty of this myself... But this is not how God would have us handle things. He tells us that "those who show mercy will have mercy shown to them." You can never go wrong with mercy, and even if people disappoint you when you have been merciful to them, our God in heaven will make it up to you.

Day 76 — March 16

DARKNESS CAN NEVER overcome the light of the Lord. And though life will always have its trials, even when we know Jesus, His light will always give hope. Faith in Jesus requires hope to latch onto, and faith is what overcomes the trials of life. "Faith is the things hoped for but not yet seen." So we have to have hope in order to have faith… Without Jesus… There's very little to hope for. Choose the light.

WE CAN LEARN from absolutely everyone. Some are simply there to show us what not to do. "The wise man learns by watching while the fool has to have a rod taken to his back." Focus on God and the good in life with passion, and the ugly stuff will fall into place. Remember that your focus is like food to what you focus on… It becomes bigger and fatter… Make sure you're feeding those things in life that are productive and positive as you choose to learn from everyone.

Day 77   March 17

HEBREWS 5:8: THOUGH He was a Son, yet He learned obedience by the things which He suffered." What an important scripture this is! Do you ever wonder why God allows things to continue in your life when they are uncomfortable, inconvenient, and even downright painful? This is why, my friends... You are learning obedience. And if you stay with your faith, it will all work towards good in the end... Hang in there.

IF THE ENEMY cannot defeat you, he will distract you!! Stay focused and do not let petty distractions pull you off your course. The world is full of glitz and glamour, and our eyes can be so easily pulled away from the things that really matter. Be intentional about what you let your eyes see and your ears hear. "God will keep in perfect peace those whose mind is stayed on Him." I don't know about you, but I would rather have perfect peace than all the bling in the world.

Day 78 — March 18

THE GOSPEL SEED once heard, never leaves. Even if it lays dormant in the heart for years, it will germinate eventually. Once someone has heard the gospel, they will have that seed in their heart, and one day it will grow. Share the gospel, and God will do the rest. "The Word of God is sharper than any two-edged sword, piercing to the division of soul and spirit" and "never comes back void."

"DISASTER PURSUES SINNERS, but the righteous are rewarded with good." As we watch the things that are going on in our country, it makes one wonder why God is allowing this... Remember that God gave man a choice, and that choice has caused many problems, but Proverbs says when you live your life with godly principles, you will be rewarded with a good life. Don't fret about the ways of the world... God's hand is on you as you seek Him. "You will only see the reward of the wicked with your eyes, but it will not come near you."

DAY 79 March 19

DECEPTION IS THE only tool that the enemy has to overcome God's people... It is imperative that we know the Word and that we stand on it no matter what things may look like!!! The enemy is actually deceiving people everywhere we look... And most of this is caused because people do not know what the Word says... And sadly, this includes Christians. "Be sober and alert because your enemy prowls around like a lion seeking whom he may devour."

"THE HARD-WORKING PERSON will always have everything he needs. He will be the first to eat the fruit of his work." "He who doesn't work, doesn't eat." There is a rampant entitlement spirit running loose in America that thinks people who have wealth should give part of what they have. That isn't what God says... You don't work... You don't eat. There are situations where people need help... And this is different, but able-bodied people should be out there working! Nobody owes anybody anything! "God blesses the work of your hands." Keep them moving!

Day 80   March 20

THE WORD LOVE is in the Bible 310 times, the word PRAY 322 times, FEAR 365 times, SERVE 122 times, but the word GIVE is in the Bible over 2,100 times! Obviously, God feels that giving is the main event... Giving is showing love, and love is what God is all about... When you choose to give, you will find blessings will overtake you because "whatever good thing you do for others, God will do for you."

THE BIBLE SAYS, "There will be terrible times ahead," and it appears we are entering those times. So how do we navigate through these terrible times? The Word also says that we are ready... Are we? Yes, if your trust is in Jesus, if your faith is mature and practiced, you will be ready. Shine your light because there are lots of people who are in the darkness, and they desperately need your light. We got this.

Day 81   March 21

THE MORE YOU think about something, the more you draw it to yourself... Spend your time thinking about what you want instead of what you don't want... Thoughts are actually the blueprints that will create your life... God tells us, "Whatever things are pure, lovely, noble, or of a good report, think on these things." Never allow your mind to run rampant with negative, chaotic, nonproductive thoughts. "Cast down wild imaginings and any thought that exalts itself above the Word of God."

MORAL DECAY IS taking place in our country. "There is a form of godliness but denying the power in their lives; have nothing to do with these people." "These people are always learning while never coming to the truth." Many universities fall into this category. Stay close to like-minded, godly people, because many will take the broad, easy path that leads to destruction. Be ready... Perilous times are at hand.

Day 82   March 22

FAITH IS NOT the same thing as positive thinking! "Faith is the substance of things hoped for, but not yet seen." Faith is the real deal, while positive thinking is the counterfeit. Always remember that the counterfeit things look exactly like the real thing… Don't fall for positive thinking unless it is coupled with your faith. "Without faith, it is impossible to please God."

LITTLE BY LITTLE can achieve greatness in every area. It is not necessary to go for the big hit. "Line by line, step by step, precept by precept." "If you're faithful with a little, you will get a lot." I absolutely love that scripture and have based my life on it as I have watched it work miracles in my life. To be thought of as being faithful is the nicest compliment you could ever pay me. Choose to be faithful… It is a choice.

Day 83 — March 23

MANY TIMES ENCOURAGEMENT will come in the form of a rebuke. A wise man hears rebuke when it has merit. A godly rebuke that corrects a personality flaw or keeps you from harm in some way is actually a golden gift... A rebuke can keep you from going through major struggles, and just seeing what happens to others in certain situations can keep you from having to go through it yourself. "The wise man learns by watching, while the fool has to have a rod taken to his back."

"I SPEAK TO them in parables, because seeing they do not see, and hearing they do not hear, nor do they understand." There are many parts of the Bible that only a true seeker of God can understand. Jesus calls it the keys to the kingdom of heaven. He says, "The treasures are given to us, but not to them," *them* referring to unbelievers. You often hear people say that the Bible does not make sense... Those people need to check their hearts and be sure they have opened their hearts and minds to Jesus. "Study to make yourself approved."

Day 84   March 24

TO DO NOTHING in the face of evil is evil itself! I grieve every time I hear a Christian say they do not want to get involved in politics... We are involved in politics!!! Whether you like it or not... And someone is fighting for you... God tells us to "occupy until He comes." It is our responsibility as biblical citizens to fight for the rights of what is right. There is a time when keeping silent is actually a sin, and when your silence causes harm to others, you become guilty along with the offender... If it is within your power to make changes where evil resides, it is your obligation to do so.

"IF ANY OF you lacks wisdom, let him ask of God, who gives to all liberally and without reproach, and it will be given to him." When you just don't know which way to turn, stop and ask God for wisdom. Just look at this wonderful promise from God!!! And then add to that, "You have not because you ask not." The only thing needed here is faith to believe you have received. Wow!!

Day 85 March 25

GOD TELLS US to "have the God kind of faith." If you believe with your whole being and truly trust that God has your back, you can speak to the mountain and tell it to be removed, and "if you believe, you will have whatsoever you say." This is not like positive thinking—that is the counterfeit—but if you couple your God-kind of faith with a positive attitude, you will have the secret.

"WHOEVER CONCEALS HIS sins will not prosper, but he who confesses and forsakes them will obtain mercy." A hidden sin is a cancer within. "Confess your sin one to the other that you might be healed." Don't go blabbing your sins to just anybody but find a trusted friend and confess your sin. Then forgive yourself and your human frailties and move on.

Day 86   March 26

YOU CANNOT LOOK ahead and move forward and still be stuck in the past; you must choose. Just remember that you cannot do anything about what has already happened, and to spend time lamenting over the past or even lengthy reminiscing over the past is purely a waste of time. A gentle reminiscent thought is sweet, but your time is now! "Forgetting those things that are behind and moving towards those things that are ahead."

THE WORLD IS a dark world, and believers are the light that will shine even brighter in the dark. Evildoers will go from bad to worse, while the children of God will be equipped to handle the terrible times ahead. God is with you even until the end. "Be strong and courageous" as you shine your light in a very dark world.

Day 87 March 27

NANCY REAGAN ONCE said, "When you're wrong, admit it, and when you're right, shut up." I have to admit that I am guilty... Be willing to admit when you have made a mistake or you are wrong... And don't gloat about being right. Always stay humble as you travel this life journey... And "be careful when you think you stand lest you fall."

SAY OUT LOUD "I do expect God to move in my life." This proclamation becomes a door of hope, and hope can cause your faith to soar. Remember that "the power of life and death is in the tongue," and when you proclaim positive thoughts out of your own mouth, it has tremendous power. Expect God to move in your life and to make the corrections needed as He causes the walls to fall that have blocked your progress.

Day 88   March 28

IF YOU DON'T forgive, you will never heal. Unforgiveness is like a cancer, and it grows! It doesn't matter what someone did to you... For your own sake, you must forgive... When you have truly forgiven, it is as if you've had the cancer removed. God knows your hurt, and He will help you to forgive when you ask Him. "Forgive others, so that you can be forgiven."

FAITH COMES FROM a dynamic relationship with God; it is born from interacting with God. Faith will only happen when certain elements come together. First of all, there must be hunger, the kind of hunger that creates a driving force. Secondly, there must be desire coupled with sincere prayer. You must really want what you are praying for. Aggression toward your prayer is counted as faith. Hunger, desire, and the expression of desire equal an answered prayer. And lastly, faith will not work unless you forgive.

Day 89 — March 29

SPEAK THE PROMISE, not the problem. "Bring Me in remembrance of My Word." Speak to the chaos and confusion in this world and remind God of His promises with your voice... "The power of life and death is in the tongue." We are living in a time where we are going to need the covenant promises of our God more than ever. Find the promises that pertain to your needs and call them out loud to God.

"YOU WILL BE like a well-watered garden, whose leaves will not wither." This is a wonderful promise from God. As a Christian, there should always be a refreshment flowing from you to others as you share your gifts... and God promises that "even in your old age, your fruit will be sweet." As I age, I love these promises... Remember that these promises are like diamonds. Claim them and remind God of what He promised, and then walk out your life and enjoy these beautiful promises.

Day 90 — March 30

CONFUSION IS NEVER from God. When you aren't sure what to do or which way to turn, sometimes the best thing to do is wait until things become clear. Your uncertainty could be because the timing is not quite right. God gives us a "sound, well-disciplined mind." I believe that when the timing is right, you will be directed in exactly what you should do. In the meantime, walk it out as God "directs your steps."

MANIPULATION OF ALL kinds is nothing short of witchcraft. I have seen Christian women manipulating their husbands, and it is very grievous. A woman of noble character looks to God and does not need to manipulate her husband or anyone else to get what she wants. Even subliminal manipulation is completely out of order. This is not God's best for us, and we will never find total joy until we do things God's way. "Make your requests be made known to God, and the peace that passes all understanding will guard your heart and your mind through Christ Jesus."

Day 91   March 31

BLESSED RESURRECTION DAY... Easter is a fun, family day, filled with good food and many memories... But don't forget the real reason for Easter is to celebrate the day that our Savior rose from the dead, "and is seated at the right hand of God, the Father, interceding for us." This is the day that represents all that we celebrate and stand for as Christians. Savor the day and be sure to give thanks to the One who made this beautiful day possible.

"THE VIEW IS always better from the high road. Choose the high road! Every choice you make affects your life either positively or negatively. Be aware of every small choice, because collectively they can set your life on a course of destruction. "Acknowledge God in all your ways, and He will make your path straight." A straight path equals gentle boundaries.

IF YOU'RE HOLDING this book, you're about to step into Bubby's house—where the coffee is strong, the limoncello is flowing, and the wisdom is served with a side of laughter. Bubby has this incredible way of making life's toughest lessons feel as simple as choosing which frog to eat first (always the ugly one, trust me). She's taught me that the wind doesn't just mess up your hair—it also brings change. And that being faithful with a little, leads to a lot...Bubby has always loved me exactly as I am, but that's never stopped her from pushing me to be better. We've laughed till we cried, sworn secrecy under the sacred "what happens at Bubby's house stays at Bubby's house" oath, and never—*never*—let these little Twerps bring us down. So, pour yourself a cup of coffee, and get ready. You're in for a ride.

– Hannah Mills, Granddaughter

 # April

Day 92 April 1

THE AREA AROUND you that you are responsible for is an externalization of who you are. Take a look at it... Is it disorderly, messy, dirty? "The walls of the sluggard lay broken." What is going on out there is what's going on in your mind. I guarantee you that if you clean up what you see, you will feel a load lifted... We serve an orderly God, and even though the phrase "Cleanliness is next to godliness" is not in the Bible... I still believe it.

THERE IS A strong current in this world, and if you are just drifting and not standing for truth, you will not end up with God. You will drift away. "The way to heaven is narrow and straight while the way to destruction is wide, and many shall go thereof." Which path are you on? Just one small deviation in a planned direction will completely change your destination... Stay on track!

Day 93 — April 2

THERE IS NO victory without a fight. There are times that "the battle belongs to God," but there are also times that we must fight our own battles, and there will be no victory if we don't stand up for what we know to be right and true and protect the innocent and our families. Be proactive, and take charge of those things that fall within your sphere of influence. "Occupy till He comes."

THERE IS NOTHING in this world that you could face that God does not have the answer for. Read the Bible and find the promises that apply to your situation, then remind God of the Scripture in prayer. The antidote is there, but you need to find it and apply it. "Bring Me in remembrance of My Word."

Day 94	April 3

THE HEAVIEST LOAD you can carry is a grudge... In fact, God tells us, "Do not let the sun go down on your wrath." That is an order from our Father in heaven, and when you carry a grudge, you are breaking that rule over and over. A grudge is unforgiveness, and if you don't forgive... God won't forgive you, and He won't even hear your prayers. Is a grudge really worth that? Give it to God... He knows your hurt.

WORDS CAN CHANGE a life... They can change a relationship... They can change the world. "The power of life and death is in your tongue." Be aware of the words you use with your loved ones and the world in general... Things that you say to a young person can affect them for the rest of their life, and marriages and friendships can be destroyed with flippant words, just as they can be enhanced with sweet, encouraging words. "A word fitly spoken is like apples of gold in settings of silver."

Day 95   April 4

WHAT WOULD YOU do if you were not afraid? Would you take a different job, move, get married? Would you start a business or write a book? Never make a decision based on fear!! God tells us 365 times in the Bible to "Fear not." It is what you do when you are afraid that will change your life and strengthen your character. "God has not given us a spirit of fear but rather a spirit of power and joy and a sound mind." Just do it!!

DO NOT LET your deficiencies identify who you are... We all have tweaks, and we should never allow them to define us, nor should we define others by their tweaks. I always say that all of us fly some sort of freak flag—some bigger flags than others—but always look past these flags to the rest of the person within. God says, "You are fearfully and wonderfully made."

Day 96 April 5

FAITH HAS A voice... Speak the Word out loud. The Word says that "Faith comes by hearing the Word of God." It is important that we hear it and not just read it. There's something powerful when you couple the Word of God with the power of the tongue. Consciously read the Word out loud as you study your Bible. Your body will follow the words, and your faith will increase.

LAWS HAVE CONSEQUENCE in life, and they also have consequences in the eternal. God has given us laws for our own good, and when we break those laws, we are putting ourselves in danger. When we do something wrong and ask God for forgiveness, He does forgive us, but we are still subject to the consequences caused by our law-breaking. "We are all to obey the laws of the land," and we are also subject to God's laws... Make a conviction to follow both. This will help to keep your boundaries gentle, both in the physical and spiritual.

Day 97 — April 6

NEVER ASSUME THAT someone you were praying for and who died did not make it to heaven… You never know the heart of someone at the moment of their death. If you were praying for someone… I believe they're in heaven! "The effectual fervent prayers of a righteous man avails much." And don't forget about "You and your household will be saved." And this would include family members. If you prayed fervently, believe you will see them in heaven.

WOULD YOU RATHER be right, or would you rather be happy? It amazes me how many people, including myself, need to be right! We hang on to our opinion, even if it means losing a loved one, a friend, or a job. When we are wrong, we need to admit it… this kind of behavior is rooted in pride, and "Pride comes before a fall." "Don't consider yourself more important than you ought." There's nothing wrong with being wrong once in a while, but it is wrong to be wrong and not admit it.

Day 98 — April 7

"DO NOT GIVE what is holy to the dogs; nor cast your pearls before swine, lest they trample them under their feet, and turn and tear you in pieces." I've always thought this Scripture was kind of harsh... but the truth is, there are people to whom you are wasting your time trying to give truth or God's Word. A better way is to live your life in such a way that they can see your truth. These rebels are God's battle... not yours.

BE GRATEFUL FOR what God has for you every single day. Celebrate your blessings every day. "You will have the needs and strength sufficient for the day." It may not be the total fulfillment, but it is the journey. Give thanks as you go along. A grateful heart will always have enough. "Delight yourself in the Lord, and He will give you the desires of your heart."

Day 99 — April 8

WE ARE TOLD 24 times in the New Testament to "be watchful." This means to pay attention to things that are going on around you and to be aware of the prophetic words coming out of the Bible. Be aware of the signs of the times, and don't just get caught up in your own little world. We all have a mission, a race to run... "Run your race, as if to win."

THE FIG TREE was the only destructive miracle that Jesus ever did, and He never did a miracle for His own benefit. Why did Jesus curse the fig tree? He acted out a parable, and a parable represents an everyday common occurrence. This parable is to show that unfruitfulness will be cut off and dried up. It didn't matter how green the leaves were or how beautiful the tree was... if it is not producing what God intended... it will be cut off... "To him that much is given, much is expected."

Day 100 — April 9

CLEVERNESS AND THE ways of men will never win the war with the evil that is rampant in the world. We need a move of God that will astound or even frighten men. The fear and reverence of God is so important, and if mankind refuses to revere God, He will bring about those things that will cause them to fear Him. This kind of fear is a total reverence and respect of an omnipotent God. "The fear of God is the beginning of wisdom."

GREATER LOVE HAS no man than this, than to lay down his life for his friends. John 15:13. Jesus willingly died on the cross for all of us. It was His choice. I pray that you have accepted this wonderful gift into your life and all the beauty, joy, and peace that come with that gift. Celebrate this day in all its glory. Eat, drink, and be merry, and remember who makes everything possible. Blessed Easter, my friends. Rejoice in the unseen.

Day 101   April 10

CHURCHILL ONCE SAID, "One of the most important components to victory is to never quit." You cannot possibly win if you quit. I believe perseverance is more important than talent. You can have all the talent in the world, but if you're not willing to push through… you will never make it. The winner of every race is the one who stayed in until the end and gave it all they had. "Run your race, as if to win."

DARKNESS COMES FROM confusion and fear. Darkness also comes from the human soul and the human heart, and this is caused by allowing your mind to go to dark places and watching and listening to things of darkness. When you set your mind on the things above and not on the things below, your mind will be enlightened, and it will remove the darkness. "Darkness cannot be with His light."

Day 102   April 11

"STOP YOUR CRYING and wipe away your tears. All that you have done for your children will not go unrewarded; they will return from the enemy's land." Jeremiah 31:16-17. I found this verse yesterday, and it is an amazing promise from God. I know that many of you have kids that have gone amuck, and here is your promise. Remind God of this promise every day! And believe you have received.

EXPERTS SAY THAT people long to know their purpose more than anything else, and that purpose is what gives people self-esteem and fulfillment. True identity comes from finding a close relationship with the One who made you, and you will never know your true identity until you know the Lord. "God promises to direct the steps of the righteous." Getting to know the Lord will guide you to your ultimate purpose, and that purpose will bring you ultimate joy.

Day 103 — April 12

SMALL OBEDIENT STEPS will eventually lead to beautiful sweeping moves. "Do not despise small beginnings." The small things in life are what bring about the large successful things in life. If you are not willing to be faithful in the small things, God will never give you the big successful things. Climb your ladder one rung at a time and don't try to skip rungs and jump to the top. "Amassed little by little, it has great value."

STAY IN CONSTANT fellowship and teaching with people who are trustworthy. There is a ton of craziness in our culture. False movements are always out there. The Word says that there will be a time of great moral decay, and I would say that we are there. It is so easy to be fooled because the counterfeits are always very similar to the real thing... prove everything by the Word of God. "Out of the mouth of two or three witnesses, a truth becomes established."

Day 104   April 13

WHEN PEOPLE FEAR and reverence God, there will be supernatural activity, as people get healed, saved, and signs and wonders appear, as well as unusual miracles. Where there is fear and reverence of God, we will witness incredible conversions of lives. And though God is not seen with the natural eye, His works become very visual. "Happy is he who fears the Lord."

EVERY CRIME COMMITTED is either committed for power, money, or lust, and yet most of the movies produced today in Hollywood glamorize these very issues. Shame on them! I encourage you to not promote their trash and boycott these wretched movies. I am convinced that much of what is going on in our culture has been instigated by movies. "Be not deceived, bad company corrupts good behavior." It doesn't say that they will be changed by our good behavior; it says that we will be corrupted by their bad behavior. Steer clear.

Day 105   April 14

"**A GENEROUS PERSON** will prosper, and anyone who gives water to another will receive a flood in return." Generosity is a principle of God, and I believe it brings more blessings on people than almost anything else we can do. If you have a want or need in any area… try giving and watch what happens to your life. And remember that giving isn't always monetary… giving comes in many forms.

FAITHFULNESS IS THE most important attribute you can have. It is the first thing you should ask God for. Faithfulness will trump every other character trait you could ever have. Be faithful even if there isn't any glory. "Many claim to have unfailing love, but the faithful person who can find?" Choose to be that faithful person.

Day 106   April 15

FAITH AND FEAR are connected. "In the fear of the Lord, there is a strong confidence." The word confidence is in reference to faith. When we have faith in God, there is a deep feeling of assurance about everything in life, and along with that, we know that God is in charge of everything, and we deeply revere Him. "Taste and see that the Lord is sweet."

"THE LORD IS faithful. He will establish you and guard you against the evil one." This is a wonderful promise given to the children of God. Hang onto this and always remind God of the things that He promised us. He tells us to remind Him… and He tells us that He will guard us against the evil in this world. "You will see it with your eyes, but it will not come near you." "As you believe, it is done unto you." "Only believe."

Day 107 — April 16

THE HOTTER THE war, the sooner the peace. Many times, when we see things really revving up, it is bringing about a finish. The last part of any hard journey always seems to be the hardest part. Stay encouraged as we see the darkness all around us in our country because it's always darkest just before dawn. And "all things done in the dark will come to light."

DECEPTION IS THE tool of the enemy. Lies are so prevalent, and they are the tool of the Antichrist… who is the father of lies. There is no time to be casual about your faith in God; our times are troubled. Pray!!!! And especially pray for our youth. Pray, in the name of Jesus, that God redeems them from the spirit of lies that has permeated our country. "Those that put their trust in God will never be disappointed." "Trust God with all your heart, and lean not on your own understanding, and God will make your paths straight."

Day 108　　　　　　　　　April 17

THE ENEMY ALWAYS tells the truth... he just doesn't tell the whole truth... remember that the enemy knows the Word of God and often uses a portion of it or takes it out of context and convinces people of a partial truth. And remember that a counterfeit looks very much like the real thing. In these end times, there will be much deception. Stay close to the Word of God. "If anyone adds to or subtracts from anything in this book, God will add to him the plagues described in this book."

YOU CANNOT PROGRESS until you decide where you are going. If you keep looking back, it will only serve to take you off course. There are times in life that you are at a crossroads, and during these times, be sure to ask God which fork in the road to take, and then keep moving, trusting that "God will direct your steps."

Day 109 — April 18

"WHEN A MAN walks in integrity and justice, happy and blessed are his children." Imagine this wonderful blessing for your children when you choose to walk in integrity! God tells us to "bring Him in remembrance of His Word," so be sure and remind God of this wonderful promise for your children. If, for no other reason, you should live a good life, it is for your children and grandchildren. "The blessings and the cursings go down even to the tenth generation."

CARES AND ANXIETIES of this life can steal from the important things in your life. God's Word tells us to "fret not, because it will only cause harm." This seems so glib when you say it because oftentimes we have a good reason to fret, but true trust in God is knowing that He has His hand on you and believing that "all things work together for good to those who love God and are called according to God's purpose for them."

Day 110 — April 19

THE WORD OF God will rise to every occasion… it will save and preserve you. Call out the promises of God whenever you feel frightened or threatened. There are over 6,000 covenant promises in the Bible, and our God is a covenant God… "Bring Me in remembrance of My Word." Remind Him of what He says, and then believe you have received.

ALWAYS GIVE YOUR best effort. It doesn't matter how old you get… as we age, we still have a calling, and our fruit should get sweeter as we get older. Just as the date trees produce their sweetest fruit as they age, this is how it should be with God's people. "We should be like a tree planted by the water that nothing will shake." "A vine that stays green." Live each day to its fullest, as you "keep your eye on the prize of your upward calling."

Day 111 — April 20

"NOT BY MIGHT, not strength but by My Spirit, says the Lord." The arm of the flesh can only do so much, but with the Spirit of God, anything is possible. If you choose to fight your own battle, you may or may not win... but if you give it to God and let Him fight your battles, you will always win. This doesn't mean that you are apathetic and ignore things... do what you can and then give it to God.

SOMETIMES THE FEARS don't go away, and you just have to go ahead and do it while you're scared. Most of life's biggest events are done by people who are frightened and still choose to go forward. God tells us to "be strong and courageous." Courage does not come naturally... it is a choice, and those courageous moments are what create success and heroes.

Day 112   April 21

THE WORD ZEAL means: like a cloak around you. It means that you are fully engaged in something. Our lives should be filled with zeal. When we undertake any project, when we are loving someone, when we are at our place of employment, when we are praying or worshiping God, even when we are enjoying a meal... everything should be done with zeal. "Whatever you do, do it as unto the Lord."

GRIEF, GUILT AND torment. Grief is a natural process, while guilt and torment are not from God. God does use a godly conviction to remind us when we do something wrong, but it has nothing to do with guilt or torment. Both of these are from the enemy. Guilt has to do with the past, and God tells us, "Forgetting those things that are behind, looking toward those things that are ahead." If Jesus is your Lord, "You are a new creature in Christ." No guilt or torment!

Day 113   April 22

THE FOUR MAJOR, awesome attributes of God are: 1. He is omnipotent, and all power belongs to Him. "Nothing is impossible with God." 2. He is all-knowing and all-wise. "His understanding is infinite." 3. He is all-good, and you can always trust Him. "He shall satisfy you with good." 4. He is totally sovereign and rules over everyone and everything. "No purpose of God can be thwarted."

THE HANDS OF God are often found at the end of our own arms. Keep your hands moving and give this invisible hand something to work with. In Hebrew, the word "hands" means the same thing as "antenna." Hands are powerful and capable of bringing in the power of God and distributing it through every aspect of your life. "God blesses the work of your hands." Be intentional in their use.

Day 114   April 23

WE ARE LIVING in a time when people are desperate for God, and it is the duty of every believer to display the works of Jesus in their lives. Depression and suicide are at an all-time high. Reach out a hand to someone in need and show them the love of the Lord. "Whatever good thing you do for others, God will do for you."

GOD TELLS US to "Open your mouth, judge righteously, defend the rights of the poor and needy." As Christians, God tells us to protect and defend those who are unable to do so themselves. To sit idly by and watch a wrong being done should never happen. Speak up and defend! Remember this: if you let a fire burn out of control, it will eventually burn to your back door...

Day 115   April 24

GOD WILL ACTUALLY magnify you when you do good for Him, even when it is unpopular. Be bold about God and don't worry about offending people. If they are turned off by you because of God, a great blessing will fall on you. This doesn't mean you should be obnoxious! "If you don't confess Me before men, I will not confess you before My Father."

THE WORD OF God tells us that Jesus will appear a second time, and we should anticipate this return with enthusiasm. The climate of our times is in perfect alignment with the return of Jesus, and that appearance will obliterate all evil, and judgment will be administered to all. It will be a day of reckoning, and no one will escape this judgment. Come, sweet Jesus.

Day 116   April 25

"GOD IS NEAR to those who call on Him." We call on Him through prayer and even just in our daily walk as we look to Him to direct our steps. It doesn't mean we have to be in a continuous posture of prayer, but we can have God on our minds with every move, and this draws Him close to us.

GOD DOES NOT take the fun out of life; in fact, He adds to it. There's nothing finer than being a Christian. My life has been so full and beautiful since I gave it over to the Lord. It is filled with love, laughter, beauty, friendship—yes, even money and blessings. There is freedom in knowing the Lord, who brings you the peace you've always longed for. "I wish above all things that you would prosper and be in good health."

Day 117   April 26

DOING THE RIGHT thing is never the wrong thing, even though it may appear to be. "Grow not weary of well-doing, because in due season you shall have your reward." Those who choose to do wrong may get by for a while, but eventually, every wrong that is done will be rewarded in kind. God created us to instinctively know the difference between right and wrong. Choose right, and right will choose you.

GOD'S TRUTH AND the trends of society are on totally different paths. "The time will come when people will not accept sound teaching." Sadly, we are experiencing this very thing as many churches are performing rather than preaching truth. Build your life on God's truth and not on society's trends. Trends come and go, leaving carnage in their wake, but God's truth will never change and will always produce good fruit.

Day 118   April 27

ANGER IS NOTHING more than a manifestation of hurt, fear, and frustration. It is imperative that we get to the root of the anger, especially when it interferes with a healthy lifestyle. When you feel anger, stop and analyze your deepest feelings to identify its cause. It often helps to share with a counselor or a trusted friend. "Confess your sins one to another that you might be healed."

THERE ARE TIMES when we ask God for something, and He answers in such a different way than we expected that we don't recognize it as His answer. Sometimes He packages things differently, and it appears He did not hear our prayer... but remember this: He hears every prayer, and He always answers. "And whatever you ask in My name, this I will do, that My Father may be glorified in the Son."

Day 119 — April 28

A PRACTICING ATHEIST believes in God but acts like an unbeliever. They are not really an atheist, but they worry, fear, and doubt. When we truly get to know God on a personal level, worry, fear, and doubt will leave. This doesn't mean that you never have any little twinges of these issues, but you learn that "God never leaves you or forsakes you," and that confidence dispels worry, doubt, and fear.

GOD HONORS THOSE who honor Him and those who are faithful in everyday matters. The little things in life make a difference to God, and He says, "If you're not faithful in the little things, then you won't be faithful in the big things." I guarantee you, if you take care of the little things as they come along, your life will stay tidy and in order. "Be faithful with a little, and you'll become ruler over much."

Day 120   April 29

DEFEAT, DEPRESSION AND doubt are common among our youth, and it is our job to encourage these young people. Times are very troubled, but remember that "God called them for a time such as this." Just as He prepared David to kill a giant and Esther to save her people, God has equipped them for these times. They do not need to hear us say how bad things are. Speak positively to them. Every generation has its giants to fight, and "God will give them the strength sufficient for the day."

ALWAYS RESPOND WITH the right thing, even when others do not acknowledge you or mistreat you. Do not retaliate! "Vengeance is mine, saith the Lord." When you do your part right and let God take care of others, He will defend you. If you decide to battle with the arm of the flesh, there's a good chance you will lose the battle. But if you let God battle it out for you, you will always win

Day 121 — April 30

HE WHO STAYS through disappointing days will win in the end. Be present and be persistent. I believe persistence is one of the best attributes an individual can possess. Stay despite doubt... stay despite persecution or trouble... persistence will often even beat a champion. Stand strong and do not waver—"He who wavers gets nothing from God."

THE REVELATION OF God in nature or elsewhere makes you accountable to God. You can see God in nature, but nature is not God. There are those who actually idolize nature itself. We are not to love the created more than we love the Creator. We serve "a jealous God," and He tells us not to put anything above Him. The First Commandment tells us to "Love God with all your heart, all your soul, and all your might, and not put anything above Him."

Haiku
My Bubby
From rags to blessings
Faithful in little and much
Now wreathed in wisdom

– Josiah Mills, Grandson

My grandma is intelligent, creative, bold, and hilarious. My favorite thing about her is her sense of humor and laughter that can make all of your problems dissipate in her presence...A real social butterfly, and she has the ability to make everyone feel like the most special person in the room, in the most authentic way...She is one of the most genuinely loving people I have ever met, and I'm so happy I was put on the Earth with her...I hope through her words in this book, you will feel The warmth and love I've had the privilege of knowing my whole life. I love you, grandma.

– Jillian Solis, Granddaughter

 # May

Day 122   May 1

GOD TELLS US 365 times in the Bible to "be strong and courageous." That accounts for one time for every day of the year. It is completely normal to be fearful when tragedy strikes, but heroism is a choice! When God tells us to "BE" courageous, it is because we are not naturally that way. Power through in times of need. It is said that a coward dies a thousand times while a brave man dies only once. "Be strong and courageous."

THERE IS A difference between faith and trust. Trust is based on knowing God's character, while faith is believing in a promise. There must be a promise before we can have faith, while trust is knowing that God loves us and will take care of us. Faith is knowing His will, while trust is knowing the love of our Father. Of course, faith and trust, coupled together, can move a mountain!

Day 123   May 2

ONE OF THE most wholesome things you can do for your life is to fear the Lord. "The fear of the Lord brings strong confidence, and your children will always be safe." Confidence means you are leaning on God, putting your hope in Him, and best of all, it promises safety for your children. The fear of the Lord is not dread but rather an enormous awe and respect as you hold Him in reverence.

NEVER MAKE A vow that you are not going to keep. "Woe to him who makes a vow he does not keep." People take vows so lightly these days, yet God warns us about this. People often wonder why their life is such a mess, and they never stop to think about what they may have done to bring it on themselves. Be careful about making vows that you cannot keep.

Day 124　　　　　　　　　　　　May 3

IN GOD'S KINGDOM, service is the greatest attribute. "To be great in the kingdom of God, you must first become servant to all." Be a servant to your loved ones, and include an undying service to those you love. Those who serve and give will always have more than enough of everything because whatever you give, God will give back to you—"pressed down, shaken together, and running over."

THE ESSENCE OF all discouragement is expecting the harvest too soon. Just as a fruit tree needs time to process the fruit and turn it into a juicy delight, so it is with God's harvest. There is a time to harvest. If you have been tending your garden of life properly, "grow not weary of well-doing, because in due season you shall have your reward."

Day 125 — May 4

YOU STEER WHERE you stare... What has your attention these days? Because those things that your eyes and ears take in are the things that you are going to move toward. I love the children's song that says: "Be careful, little ears, what you hear, and be careful, little eyes, what you see." God tells us to "keep your thoughts on the things above and not on the things below."

THE GRACE OF God is given as needed. Today's grace cannot be administered for tomorrow. "You will have the grace sufficient for the day." And just like the manna given to the Israelites on a daily basis, which could not be gathered beforehand or saved, such is God's grace. On the day you need it, it will always be there.

Day 126 — May 5

A STEWARD OF God must be found faithful. You cannot call yourself a servant of God if you can't be depended upon or trusted. If I could only have one word to describe me, I would want it to be "faithful." When I make my journey to heaven, I pray that I will hear those coveted words: "Well done, good and faithful servant."

WE ARE CALLED to faithfulness rather than greatness, and many of our good works will not only go unnoticed but may even seem to turn against us. However, *"Be not deceived. As a man sows, so shall he reap."* Just as poor choices eventually bring consequences, good, fair, ethical, and kind choices will also yield rewards. No matter how things may appear, *"Grow not weary in well-doing, for in due season, you shall have your reward."* That's a promise!

Day 127 — May 6

NEGATIVE THOUGHTS WILL never lead to positive results! God tells us to "think on whatever is true, right, lovely, noble, pure, excellent, praiseworthy, or of a good report." Remember that thoughts are the blueprints for life. Keep your thoughts positive and "cast down any wild imaginings that try to exalt themselves above the word of God."

PEOPLE WILL ALWAYS listen to a testimony from someone who has faced challenges. No one wants to hear only about how wonderful your life has always been—it can be discouraging to them. But when you share what you've been through and how you have overcome it, that becomes a powerful testimony that can inspire others. Share your story with honesty and transparency. Be an overcomer, no matter what you face. *"We overcome the enemy by the blood of the Lamb and the word of our testimony."*

Day 128   May 7

WE DO NOT need to spend hours explaining our feelings to God because He knows every single detail about us. "He knows every single hair on our head." He knows every fear and worry, and He knows our most intimate thoughts. "God knows our needs even before we ask." Trust Him and "only believe."

STAY IN THE boundaries that God has set and keep building. God has framed boundaries around a life that trusts Him. It is like having an umbrella over you when it rains. Stay under the umbrella, and it will keep you on the holy highway that God has provided for His people, a highway that no evil thing may come upon. "Those who put their faith in God will never be disappointed."

Day 129 — May 8

SALVATION DOES NOT require anything except your belief and confession that Jesus is Lord. There is absolutely nothing else you can do to earn salvation—it is the beautiful, free gift of God. "The wages of sin is death, but the gift of God is eternal life." He made it so easy, yet there are those who will still perish because they refuse this precious gift. There is nothing that can purchase this gift. It is free. "Only believe."

NEVER GIVE UP on your race, even if you have to crawl to the finish line. Keep the faith and keep going. Finish your race, whether it be a glorious, flag-waving finish or one where you barely make it—but make it across that finish line and do not waver in your faith. "Run your race as if to win."

Day 130   May 9

IT IS SO important that we remember that choices are what make the world go round. People always say, "God's in control," and He is, but don't forget He gave that control to us. He gave us the right to choose. So even when we pray for somebody, we have to pray that their choice will change. "I lay before you life and death, blessing and cursing... Choose life."

DON'T WASTE THE experience you're going through by denying it, hiding from it, or getting bitter or angry about it. In many cases, wouldn't you rather learn the lesson only once? Rather than becoming defensive and blaming other people for your own insecurities, maybe you should stop and examine what it is that bothers you so much—and learn from the situation. "Count it all joy when you go through fiery trials because it is perfecting you."

Day 131   May 10

THERE ARE TIMES God will allow what He hates to accomplish what He loves. God never causes bad things to happen, but He often uses them. You can usually see God's thumbprint on things when He is involved. Keep an eye out for Him in the midst of your trials and "count it all joy as you go through the fiery trials because it is perfecting you."

WHAT YOU LOVE will determine how you live. Check your life for what you love. This is not an insignificant suggestion—it is necessary for you to proceed toward the goal that God has planned for you. "God has a good plan for your life, a plan to prosper you and not to harm you." "The love of money and stuff is the root of all evil." Note that it's not money that is the root of all evil; it is the "love of money." Guard your heart and where you place your love with all diligence.

Day 132   May 11

PROVERBS SAYS THAT the word of God is "healing to your flesh and refreshment to your bones." Remind God of this when you're feeling unwell. He tells us to remind Him of what He says. "Healing to all of your flesh." I don't know about you, but I like that one! Just one more good reason to make sure you are reading the word of God. "Study to make yourself approved."

EVEN IN OLD age they will still produce fruit; they will remain vital and green." God tells us to remind Him of what He says, and I am reminding Him of this one! Even in old age—I just love that! I'm there, my vine is still green, and my hair is not gray. And I pray that I am producing sweet fruit.

Day 133 — May 12

NOT ONE SPARROW falls to the ground without God knowing. Do not worry for yourself, because if God cares about the sparrow, how much more does He care for you? Everything that happens to us is known by God. No one can harm us unless God allows it. Trust Him with all your heart.

BENEVOLENT DETACHMENT! ARE there people in your life that you love, but it just seems there is always a problem with them? You aggravate them, or they aggravate you? Some of these people you need to say goodbye to, and others you just need to stay detached from, even as you intermingle with them. "As iron sharpens iron, so the countenance of a friend sharpens a friend." Friction between people can be healthy, but in some cases, a benevolent detachment is necessary. Love them, but stay detached.

Day 134   May 13

ALWAYS REMEMBER THAT even though many things are completely impossible for men, "nothing is impossible for God." If you have a dream that has not come to fruition for many years, and it seems impossible that it ever will—never give up! God can do anything for those who believe.

THERE IS A flood of filthiness that is trying to sweep our youth away, but the flood of God is a flood of cleansing, and He cannot be outflooded. God is going to rescue our youth. Pray for the river of God to overflow. It is said that if the enemy could get one generation, he could take down the whole world. But always remember: "What is impossible with man is possible with God." Pray for our youth and our country

Day 135   May 14

WHEN THE RIGHTEOUS cry out to God, He hears them and rescues them. We need to be crying out to God for our country and our children! Statistics say that over half of our children have anxiety, depression, or some sort of mental disorder. And this, my friends, is the result of a godless culture. They don't need a pill or an antidepressant—they need God and our prayers! Pray!!!

IT IS NOT easy to do what is right when it brings pain on you, but God will bring miracles upon you when you choose to do what is right in difficult situations. We instinctively know right from wrong. Always choose to do what you know to be right, even when no one is looking, because God never misses a thing. It's what you do when no one is looking that sets apart those who are successful from those who fail. "You will know them by their works."

Day 136   May 15

THE WORD OF God tells us: "If we pray one for the other, we will be healed." One of the best things you can do is to pray for people. This opens this promise wide open for you. Remind God when you feel unwell that you have been that person who prays for others, and therefore you know that He is going to "hasten to lift you off your sickbed."

BE RESPONSIBLE FOR your own life and humbly ask for what you can't do. A know-it-all will never learn anything! God's word says, "The wise man learns by watching, while a fool has to have a rod taken to their back." If you are not willing to learn from others, you will have to learn the hard way. Be open to instruction.

Day 137   May 16

GOD WILL REVEAL secrets to those who revere and fear Him... "Things you do not know." He will show you "hidden treasures in dark secret places." And He will give you creative ideas... Stay alert and expectant as you walk out your journey with God "directing your steps."

BE DETERMINED TO be happy in life... and it is not about money and "stuff" either; it is about choosing to be happy inside. There will always be ugly stuff and ugly people to deal with, and if you allow this criterion to determine your happiness, you will waver and be unstable in all your ways. Decide to be happy! Not because of people, stuff, the weather, or your finances, but because God and His promises are the source of your joy!! "Seek ye first the kingdom of God and His righteousness, and all other things shall be added unto you."

Day 138   May 17

LIFE ISN'T ALWAYS a bowl of cherries... In fact, some days you feel like crap... But God promises, "Though there may be tears at night, joy will come in the morning." This simply means that "this too shall pass." Don't lament over an off day... do what you can to make your day easier and trust God, that in the morning there will be joy and you will feel better.

KNOW YOUR GOALS and start somewhere. Take the first step. Set your goal, and once you have determined that you're going to the top of the ladder, only focus on your next step, or you can become discouraged. As you climb your ladder of success, take time to celebrate each small victory along the way... Acknowledge God as you go, and one day you'll find yourself at the top looking down. "The diligent hand shall rule." "Those who put their trust in God will never be disappointed."

Day 139   May 18

GOD WILL BLESS and honor those who fear Him. But departing from the fear of the Lord does not only bring evil snares into your life, but that evil will drop down to your offspring. The fear of the Lord is to hate and depart from evil. It isn't always a parent's fault when a child goes amok, but many times it is… "The sins of the father come down even to the tenth generation." Always remember, when you do something wrong, you're not only bringing a curse on yourself, but you are bringing it down on those who come behind you.

A VICTIM MENTALITY is so disgusting, and when people whine and cry about their life and their issues and their pain, financial situation, their divorce, their husband… and on and on and on, it does not help to get more pity… On the contrary, it turns people off and they push the victim away. There is a choice involved… Do you want to be a victim or do you want to be a victor? The same problems exist with both… but one wallows in the problems, and one overcomes… "I can do all things through Christ, who strengthens me." Get hold of that promise… Repeat it every time you want to whine and become a victor instead of a victim.

Day 140   May 19

"PROFESSING THEMSELVES TO be wise, they became fools." I can't tell you how many times I've thought of this proverb as of late. Where is just plain old common sense? The colleges sure aren't teaching it. Most things in life don't take college to figure out... but rather just common sense and integrity... "God made a man upright, but he has devised many schemes." Pray for our youth... They are truly troubled.

DON'T JUST SERVE God with your hands... Serve Him with your heart as well. Remember that God looks at the heart, and He reminds us that "obedience is better than sacrifice." As New Testament Christians, we are not required to make sacrifices, but we are required to obey and stay within the perimeters that God has set for all mankind. These perimeters are for our own good... Stay on that "holy highway" that God has provided, where no evil thing can travel

Day 141　　　　　　　　　　　May 20

YOUR WORDS HAVE power... They are like a two-edged sword that can either bring life or death... They can set your life on a path of destruction, or they can speak hope into the life of a child... Never take your words lightly, and be diligent when choosing the ammunition that comes out of your mouth... "The power of life and death is in the tongue."

"DO NOT BOAST about tomorrow, for you do not know what a day may bring." Life can change in a moment's time, and we need to live in the moment and appreciate today. Tomorrow is not guaranteed, and yesterday is just a memory. Wake up every morning and act as if it is your last day... because it could be.

Day 142   May 21

EVERYTHING NEEDED FOR spiritual life is found in Jesus… "Taste and see that He is good." Once you know the true goodness of a heart surrendered to Jesus, you could never go back… God says, "He will give you a new heart." Acceptance of Jesus in your life can and does change your life. A depth and a softening of the heart is evident to all who knew you before.

OUR GOD IS the God of faithfulness who is infinitely, unchangingly true… He never changes His mind, He never lies, He always forgives you when you ask, and He shows mercy beyond anything any of us deserve. I truly pity those who have spent their life never knowing their Creator… My God is everything to me, and my prayer is that everyone would have "the peace that goes beyond understanding" when you know your Lord. "Draw close to Him, and He will draw close to you."

Day 143   May 22

"ABIDE IN ME and I in you." Too often, people are saved, but they do not have a living relationship with Jesus. He tells us that just as a branch cannot bear fruit unless it is connected to the vine, so it is with our relationship with Jesus. There is a richness to life when we are connected to our Creator... Abide, or live, in Him!

OFT TIMES YOU don't know the value of a moment until it becomes a memory. We often take those precious moments for granted, and then we look back and realize that the moment was magical, and we missed it until it was over. Live in the moment and revel in the details. "This is the day the Lord has made; I will rejoice and be glad in it."

Day 144   May 23

THERE ARE DAYS in life that we feel discouraged, and it seems that nothing is going right... I find that during those times, if I stop and remember the times in my past that God brought me through something very difficult, it will encourage me... "We overcome the enemy by the blood of the Lamb and the word of our testimony." Sometimes we need to hear our own testimony.

I SEE PEOPLE struggling through life, and the interesting part is they aren't willing to fight for things. They call themselves losers and give up. If you are to be successful in life, you must be willing to fight for what you want. To work hard... To keep your nose to the grindstone... To do things you don't want to do... "The diligent hand shall rule." Be diligent and go for it!

Day 145   May 24

GIVE WHAT YOU wanna get... You want love, give love... You want mercy, give mercy... You need money, give money... Whatever you give is what will come back to you. Whether you give good or bad, it will come back to you. "Pressed down, shaken together, and running over." If you give by the spoonful, you get spoonfuls back... If you use a bucket to give, you get bucketfuls back.

I BELIEVE IN divine providence... When you find yourself in a strange predicament, look for God's fingerprint. "God works in mysterious ways." And sometimes, when you least expect it, God will intervene in your life. Watch for Him in delays, changes of direction, new people, new words, and anything else that is out of the ordinary. Changes of any kind are often opportunities presented by God.

Day 146 — May 25

"IT IS THE goodness of God that draws them to repentance." It is not about fearmongering, or telling people that the end of the world is at hand... or telling them that they're going to burn in hell 🔥. It is telling them about the goodness of God that draws them in... When others see you walk in the peace that only Jesus can give, and they see your integrity and kindness... this is what draws them to God.

JESUS SAYS TO "speak to the mountain and tell it to be removed, and if you believe in your heart, you shall have whatsoever you say." And directly following that statement, He says, "Forgive that you might be forgiven." "When you stand praying, forgive, that God may hear your prayers." I believe that we miss out on many answered prayers because of unforgiveness... "Do not let the sun go down on your wrath."

Day 147 — May 26

OFT TIMES, BREAKTHROUGH is not an event but rather a process, and I see people missing it as they look for an event and then dismiss the happenings because they're not realizing that the process is leading up to the event. "There's a time and season for everything under the sun," and the process season is equally as important as the actual harvest. "Grow not weary in well-doing, because in due season, you shall have your reward."

THERE ARE SOME things in life that you're just not gonna get. God blesses you in so many ways, but there are still things that you're just gonna have to live without. Make a decision to embrace the things that have landed within your parameters… Go forward and try to achieve the things you long for, but be willing to love what is yours. "In all things give thanks."

Day 148   May 27

SWEET MEMORIES ARE precious and can take us back to things that are sweet... But memories can also be a minefield of things that are not so sweet and can even rob our joy... While memories are part of life, God tells us to "forget the things that are behind and look towards the things that are ahead." I liken it to the rearview mirror... Keep your eyes on the road ahead and only glance in the rearview mirror.

WE ALL HAVE to deal with an interrupted life at one time or another. When you find yourself at one of these interruptions, trust God to direct your new course of action and listen for that "still, quiet voice that says, 'Stop. Go this way.'" And remember that He often uses people to give you direction... a word spoken that confirms a witness in your own spirit. Stay open! "Behold, I do a new thing."

Day 149   May 28

MOST OF THE time when we do something that we shouldn't be doing and are sorry for, it is often our environment that causes it... The people you hang around with and the things that are going on around you will make the difference in how you live your life... "Be not deceived, bad company corrupts good behavior." Change your environment, change your life.

PRIDE WILL COST you everything and then leave you with nothing! "Pride comes before destruction, and a haughty spirit before a fall." Pride can look like confidence, superiority, importance, or intelligence, but it is actually lethal! And in the end, it leads to destruction. It is wonderful to recognize your worth and to display confidence, but this can be a slippery slope... Stay humble. "Let another man praise you, and not your own mouth; a stranger, and not your own lips."

Day 150   May 29

DO THE THINGS you dread doing first… I call this "Eat the ugly frog first." When you have something that needs to be done and you procrastinate, it wastes precious energy as you fret over it. I always say that the ugly frog tastes horrible going down, but it leaves you very satisfied when you're done. "All hard work brings profit, but mere talk leads to poverty." Eat the ugly frog!

WHEN WE HAVE God on the inside of us, we have a treasure inside. We do not need earthly treasures, although they are also available to us, but God has filled us with a treasure chest of jewels that we need to embrace and share. When you have called out the name of Jesus, He lives in your heart, and if this isn't a treasure chest, I don't know what is. "At that day, you shall know that I am in my Father, and you in me, and I in you."

Day 151   May 30

THERE ARE SOME doors in your life that will only open with gentleness... "A gentle answer turns away wrath." There are times that we need to come out swinging, but many times it is that "sweet, gentle spirit" that will move the mountain in front of you... "It is God's loving kindness working through you that draws others to repentance." Play nice.

THE ROOT WORD of miserable is miser... Are you aware that studies have proven that generous people who give to others rarely, if ever, have any kind of mental disorders? And not only that, the word "give" is in the Bible more than any other word. "Give, and it shall be given to you, pressed down, shaken together, and running over shall men give unto your bosom." Giving is the best antidepressant or tranquilizer you can take.

Day 152   May 31

"IN THIS LIFE you will have trouble," but God will see you through. Life is like a roller coaster with its ups and downs, and even extreme lows and highs... But God promises us that He will walk through every single trial that life can throw at us. Look to Him and trust Him with all your heart, and He will always bring you out safely to the other side of trouble.

THERE ARE LOTS of good people in the world, even though our news media gives attention to those who are not good. Do not get caught up in the division that is being pushed on us, with the implication that people are not good... This is just not true... "Do not lose heart." There are tons of good people out there. "Love your neighbor as you love yourself."

My Grandma
is Smart as whip,
And shoots from the hip...
A warrior of God,
Captain of the ship...
Beautiful and wise
Inside and out,
Even Demons flee when they hear her shout...
A spiritual guru and master of prayer,
She holds the key in her full head of hair...
So, make this book part of your daily life,
And surely, you'll prosper with the treasures you'll find...
Love you Grandma!

– Thomas Solis Grandson

 # June

Day 153 June 1

"BY HIS STRIPES we are healed." If you can believe that and not waver, you are healed! Do not take the promises of God lightly... Find them in the Bible, memorize them, and call them out to God... Our God is a covenant God, and when He makes a promise, He keeps it! "Has He not said it and will He not do it?"

PEOPLE WILL FAIL you, but God will never let you down. You are never alone when you know God. "God will never leave you or forsake you." I am amazed how even though I live alone, I always feel that someone is in the house with me. I constantly remind myself that there is no one there. There comes a time in a mature relationship with God that you realize you have a constant companion and you are never lonely. Thank you, Jesus.

Day 154   June 2

PEOPLE ARE NOT showing off!! They are sharing happy moments and achievements, unless you are viewing from a jealous point of view… I have friends that I hesitate to share the good things in my life with because I feel they are not happy for me… "Where there is envy and jealousy, there is also every other evil working." Share your life with those who wish you well…

THERE ARE UNSAVORY unlovable people that we meet every day, and some of them are even in our own family. These people may never change and it is possible that they will die in their folly. Love them anyway and show them kindness because we never know when our acceptance of them just the way they are, could be the thing that draws them to God. "It is God's loving kindness working through us that draws them to repentance."

Day 155 — June 3

THE BEST LIES are often close to the truth... Remember that a counterfeit looks very much like the real thing. And lies always have just enough truth in them to make them believable. But remember, "Satan is the father of lies." And he knows the Word of God and will often twist it and use it as a counterfeit... When we are filled with the Spirit of God, He will whisper truth in our ears. Listen for that still small voice that says, "Stop, go this way."

"BEHOLD, I WILL do a new thing, now it shall spring forth; shall you not know it? I will even make a road in the wilderness and rivers in the desert." Somebody needs to hear this today. A new thing!!! Be expectant as you walk out your days. Look for and embrace subtle changes that could easily be overlooked.

Day 156 — June 4

NO MATTER WHAT you are doing or where you are in your life, this will come to an end... Whether it be troubled times or the peak of joy... The end is coming... Revel in the moment if it is good, "This is the day the Lord has made, I will rejoice and be glad in it"... and stand patient if it's troubled because this too shall pass. "Though there may be tears at night, joy will come in the morning."

THE WORD FAITHFUL means that others can completely trust you, and you can always be depended upon. I personally don't think there is any other word that is more complementary than to be thought of as faithful. The words "Well done, good and faithful servant" are coveted by all who are heaven-bound. A faithful character is worth more than silver and gold, and it is available to all who choose this valuable attribute.

Day 157   June 5

IF YOU ARE not faithful and wise with worldly things, you will not be faithful with Godly things..." Those who are faithful will find true riches in this life, and then when they enter into God's kingdom, they will hear those coveted words, "Well done, good and faithful servant."

WHATEVER SKILLS YOU have, God will use to help others. Your experiences, even the bad experiences, can be used to minister to others. The good, the bad, and the ugly... In fact, the uglier the experience, the more powerful the testimony. When needy people realize that you have been through things that they are dealing with, they are more apt to receive from you... Be transparent as you share your testimony. "We overcome the enemy by the blood of the Lamb, and the word of our testimony."

Day 158 — June 6

ANGER AND UNFORGIVENESS can nullify your prayers. God's Word says, "When you stand praying... forgive, or God does not hear your prayers." Imagine the heavy price of forfeiting your prayers just to hold on to anger!! I know there are times that you have been totally hurt... And God knows what you've been through... Your part is to tell God to help you to forgive. This does not mean that you have to approve of the individual or that you ever even have to be around them again... But you do have to forgive them. God will put it in your heart when you ask Him. And remember, He tells us to "pray for those who have mistreated us"... Do it God's way... It works.

THE TWO MOST important days of your life are the day you're born and the day you realize why. We are all born with a good plan for our life, but unfortunately, many never discover what that plan is. This plan must be sought after and searched for just as you search for gold or silver. There is a plan that God has ordained for you from the beginning of your days. "For I know the plans I have for you, declares the Lord, plans to prosper you and not to harm you, plans to give you hope and a future." If you honor God, He will direct you towards this coveted future.

Day 159   June 7

BE PREPARED FOR what comes next in your life… While it is important to live in the moment, it is wise to be prepared… Do not put your head in the sand and refuse to see things. "Watch the ant, it stores its provisions in summer and gathers its food at harvest"… Consider how you use your resources, because "Where you put your treasure, there the desires of your heart will also be."

SOMETIMES CERTAIN ISSUES stem from a spiritual problem and can only be quieted by a move of God. Jesus told His disciples about a stubborn issue, "This kind will only come out by prayer and fasting." If you have faithfully prayed and not seen any changes, try fasting as you pray. If Jesus said it… it is true! Fast and pray!

Day 160   June 8

A PERSON WHO has experience will never be at the mercy of an argument. 'Been there, done that' has a lot of truth to it... Every decade of life has its own set of challenges, and I know that many dread getting older, but honestly, it has so much merit... "Even in old age, they will produce fruit, and they will remain vital and green"... I love that the Date trees in our desert produce sweeter fruit as they get older... I claim that for myself.

"THE FIRST TO speak seems right until someone comes forward and cross-examines." Only a fool listens to one side of a story and presumes it to be right. Always be willing to listen to others, even when they don't agree with what you think. We often say that we have researched something, when, in fact, we've only researched things that agreed with what we believe. The wise man keeps his mind open as he considers both sides of the story.

Day 161

June 9

WHEN YOU SEE someone that you care about doing something that you know is going to bring them harm... Tell them! It can be hard, and they may not even like it... But I believe that a true friend tells a friend when they see a disaster ahead... "Two are better than one because they can help each other succeed." And be willing to listen to the wise counsel of a friend or loved one. A friend in need is a friend indeed.

YOU CAN DO a lot for God after you have prayed, but you cannot do anything for God until you have prayed. Prayer is our communication with God, and we know how life is without good communication... "The effectual fervent prayers of a righteous man avails much." And I love the one that says, "You have not because you ask not." Don't sit around whining and complaining about things if you've not bothered to communicate with your Father. Just saying.

Day 162   June 10

GOD DOES NOT call the equipped… He equips the called. There are many times in a Christian's life when we feel inadequate to do something that we know God would have us do… But I know from experience that if you step out and start the process, God will give you the ability. "Be prepared whether the time is favorable or not. Patiently correct, rebuke, and encourage others."

WHEN WAS THE last time you did something for the first time? As people age, it seems to be the natural inclination to cling to the things that you've always done. And yet it is so refreshing to experience something new, whether it be a taste you've never tried, a vacation in a different spot, a walk on a new path, even a new hairdo, or an outfit you would've never worn before… I encourage you this day to try something new… "Forgetting those things that are behind and looking towards those things that are ahead." "Behold, I do a new thing."

Day 163   June 11

"ANGER IS CRUEL and wrath is like a flood, but jealousy is even more dangerous." Jealousy is a form of hate that is rooted in insecurity... Check your heart to be sure that you are not operating in this dangerous zone... it is natural to desire things that others have, and this is a compliment, but be sure your desires stay away from jealousy wherein "Lies every other evil working."

THE WHOLE WORLD is going from order to disorder. This is the natural process of this world, as the earth is passing away. All of this mayhem has been recorded and prophesied in the Bible. The scripture "fear not" is in the Bible 365 times. One for every day of the year... So do not be afraid of what we see with our eyes because God is still in control, contrary to the way things may look... Hold the world and the things in it loosely... Have fun but hold it loosely. "Only the things of God will last."

Day 164 — June 12

THE QUICKEST ROUTE to freedom from sin is confession! "Confess your sins one to the other that you might be healed." Never keep dark things in the dark, because that is where they grow... "Darkness cannot be where there is light." And one small match can light up a whole room... Put light on negative situations and they must flee...

IT IS NOT circumstances that thwart your progress through life, but it is rather your attitude that hinders the success of your joy. Circumstances come and go, and change negatively and positively constantly. It is said that 90% of success in life is attitude, and only 10% circumstances... Do what you know to do to correct any negative circumstances as you make a conscious decision to enjoy and learn from the journey. "In whatever state you find yourself, be content." This too shall pass.

Day 165 — June 13

"WEEPING MAY ENDURE for a night, but God's favor is for a lifetime." To have God's favor on you is the most powerful blessing that you could ever receive! Pray his favor over yourself, your children, and all those that you love... This is the sweetest prayer there is... In Jesus' name. Amen.

WE ARE ALL called to carry out our calling. Every single person is called to a ministry of some sort. Sometimes it is simply serving your family, but whatever it is, pour yourself out and bless your family or your very specific and individual ministry to your fullest measure. Every ministry is important. Pour out the best that you have. "Do everything as unto the Lord." Life is so good when you do it right!

Day 166 — June 14

THERE IS NOTHING more evocative than the sound of doors opening and closing... nothing more hopeful and nothing more final... I often ask God to open and shut doors, symbolic for the beginning and end of something. Ask God to open new doors of opportunity and slam doors that are unproductive, and then "forget those things that are behind, and look to those things that are ahead."

LOVE WITHOUT TRUTH is hypocrisy, but truth without love is brutality. "Faithful are the wounds of a friend, profuse are the kisses of an enemy." Sometimes truth can hurt, but it is also helpful when shared in love. Always stay open to a truth when it is shared by someone who loves you. Never reject a truth that can help you. "The wise man will hear counsel and increase his learning."

Day 167   June 15

IF YOU WEAR a cross, or place it beautifully on a wall, or even hang a shiny trinket in your car... Pay attention to what it truly means to you... it represents your passport to the heavenly realm... Do not conform to the culture that is literally killing mankind, but rather remember your savior as you acknowledge the deep, pure meaning of the cross. "Jesus died for the sins of mankind." Honor him with gratitude and reverence...

THE FURNACE OF affliction is very real, and all of us will go through trials and suffering in this life. Suffering can either lead to a building of your faith or it can take you down. It is a choice. But be assured that there is no problem or affliction that is too big for God, and he has made a provision for anything you could possibly go through. "God gives you strength sufficient for the day." Find a promise in the Bible and apply it to your situation..."Count it all joy when you go through the fiery trials because it is perfecting you."

Day 168   June 16

WHEN YOU FIND yourself getting weary, and your life has become boring or dull, don't just muddle through life... Make it an adventure! Challenge yourself in some way, and you will find that the mundane things in life will become exciting. "This is the day the Lord has made... Rejoice and be glad in it."

BE GENTLE WITH the flaws of others, because every single person flies some sort of a freak flag, including you! "God promises that he will finish the work He has started in all of us." There are some people that we cannot abide by their individual flaws, and in that case, we do not have to hang around with them, but we should not judge them because their freak flag is different than ours. "Get the board out of your own eye before you try to pick the speck out of your brother's eye."

Day 169   June 17

AS A CHILD of God, we have an inheritance... God has given us time, treasures, and talents as well as over 6000 promises in the Bible... There are many who waste or ignore their inheritance... Recognize and be grateful for the treasures that God has allotted to your life..." Godliness with contentment has great gain." And "Run your race as if to win."

PEOPLE IN OUR culture are used to a life of emptiness. Empty calories, empty movies, empty conversation, even empty church services. Fill your life with the sweetness of God's word and be an example. "Taste, and see that the Lord is sweet, blessed is he who hopes in him." Serving God is such a fulfilling life. The things of God are never empty and "his word never comes back void."

Day 170 — June 18

YOUR CHOICES HAVE natural consequences, and you will have to deal with them. God will always forgive you when you ask, but his forgiveness does not remove the consequences. Every single choice has a consequence relevant to that choice... Be cognizant of your choices as you walk out your journey... "The word of God is a lamp unto my feet and a light upon my path."

"HE WHO FEARS has not been made perfect in the love of God." Fear has torment, and in the presence of God, there is no torment. I know we live in the flesh and there are times that fear will grip us, but when that happens, be sure and call out to God. I simply say "Jesus" out loud. We still have human frailties, and we desperately need our Lord. "Call unto me and I will deliver you from all your fears."

Day 171 — June 19

ANGELS ARE MOTIVATED by God's word and when we speak the word of God. "The Voice of God divides the flames of fire." Speaking God's word audibly is actually God's voice, and it can not only bring angels on the scene, but it also has the power to move the mountains in your life.

GOD PROMISES HIS people rewards. Some feel we are not supposed to desire rewards, and yet God promises us rewards. "God is a rewarder of those who diligently seek him." It is not only okay to look for rewards, but we should look for and expect them. When you see those who are blessed, you are seeing those who diligently seek him. You cannot earn salvation, but you can earn rewards.

Day 172 — June 20

JESUS IS THE most famous man who ever lived, and whether you consider him to be God or not, there is no denying that his notoriety has filled the earth with magical wonder... and yet the 33 years that he came to live on the earth as a man, he chose to be a servant..."Those who are to become great in the kingdom of God must first become servant to all." Serve someone today.

SET YOUR MIND to be happy and to see the good in every situation. There are tons of things around us that are not good, and we can choose to fill our heads with these visions, or we can choose to see the good... It is our choice... And what we choose to see will impact our lives positively or negatively. "Whatever things are pure, whatever things are true, whatever things are lovely or beautiful, if there be any virtue or anything noble, think on these things."

Day 173   June 21

THE WISDOM AND knowledge of God are so vast, and the ways of the Lord are mysterious and dynamic…Man will never understand God's ways, but as we become familiar with our Father, we become aware of him in every little detail of our life…We learn to trust him and believe that he is "directing our steps." There is no greater comfort in my life than this…" My thoughts are not your thoughts, neither are your ways my ways," declares the Lord.

THE DEVIL USES unforgiveness to get people under his power. Anger is the biggest problem that we have in our lives. Make a decision to forgive. Once you make the decision, God will do the rest… You don't have to feel like you have forgiven them; you just have to do it. And then pray for them and let God work in you the forgiveness that you have confessed out loud. "When you stand praying, forgive, or God does not hear your prayer."

Day 174   June 22

WHEN YOU MAKE decisions to do something, make every effort to carry out your plan, even if things don't look perfect, or you're troubled by things. There are always things that are going on, and if you wait until things are perfect, you will never get things done ... life is filled with problems, and honestly, you can always find a reason to procrastinate. I am a firm believer of 'where there is a will, there is a way.' "Whoever watches the wind will not plant; whoever looks at the clouds will not reap."

DO NOT BECOME a victim of regret. Like shame, regret is a waste of time, and God does not use shame or regret to correct His children. Instead, He uses conviction—a gentle urging when we are doing something that displeases Him or may harm us. Conviction does not bring grief, shame, or anxiety. Once you have done what you can to make restitution for past mistakes, turn the page and move forward.

Day 175   June 23

THERE ARE TIMES that we are doing everything right and making all the right choices... But our heart is out of sorts... Others may not see our error because outwardly we are doing all the right things... But remember, "Men look at the outward appearance, but the Lord looks at the heart." Stop often and check the motive of your heart, because "the issues of life flow from the heart."

THE WORD "BUT" means in strong contrast to something. When the word "but" precedes a statement, it is often to negate what was just said, or used to make a stronger statement about the topic. It can also be used as a cop-out... God says to "let your yea, be yea, and your nay be nay." Be careful how you use the word "but."

Day 176 — June 24

ALWAYS TAKE THE right action, even if you do not know the outcome...We ought to be people who always do what we know to be right...In the end, the right choice is always the good choice. We know instinctively right from wrong..." God created man in his own image." and that image was perfect... "But man has devised many schemes."

"I CAN DO all things through Christ, who strengthens me." Do you really believe that? And if you do, why haven't you attempted to do more things? Most of us have gifts that we've never even tapped into. If you don't try something, you will never know. If there is something that you've always wanted to do, and you've never tried it, give it a shot! And by the way, Grandma Moses was 77 years old when she painted her first painting. 'No guts, no glory.'

Day 177   June 25

THERE ARE OVER 2000 fears known to mankind and yet we are only born with 2 fears... The fear of loud noises, and the fear of falling... All other fears are learned! I love the promise that says "call unto me and I will deliver you from all of your fears." This works! And I know this from personal experience... I was riddled with fears growing up... And today the only fear I have is not pleasing the Lord... Call to Jesus...

YOU CAN DOWHAT'S right whether you feel like doing it or not. We all know right from wrong... Good from bad... Black from white... And it doesn't matter whether we feel like believing it or not... It is just the way it is... So no matter what your feelings are... Always choose to do the right thing! Because your decisions matter, and will impact your life. "Be not deceived, as you sow you shall reap."

Day 178 — June 26

"THE FEAR OF God is the beginning of wisdom." It is not just to believe that God is real...there is so much more to it than that...To recognize his omnipotence and the power of God, is as important as believing he is our healer, provider, protector and our Heavenly Father...Never be flippant about God..."Fear God and keep his commandments for this is the whole duty of man."

"PLEASANT WORDS ARE like a honeycomb, sweetness to the soul and health to the bones." According to this proverb, sweet words can be healthy... Use your voice in such a way that it is a calming comfort rather than a sword that pierces the heart of others. Be intentional in the tone of your voice, even if you are reprimanding or disputing an issue. People will listen to what you have to say when your voice is calm. "Sweet words are like apples of gold."

Day 179   June 27

GOD WILL USE our hardships to bring the best out of us... Life is filled with many twists and turns, ups and downs... And every single experience is a life lesson that can be used to elevate everything about you. "Count it all joy when you're going through the fiery trials because God is perfecting you."

THE WORD "GIVE" is in the Bible, over 1500 times! That is more than the word love, pray, or faith. When we give, we open the windows of heaven over ourselves. God loves a giver! If you really want to be blessed, learn to give of your stuff, and yourself. You can never outgive God, and "whatever you give will be given back to you, pressed down, shaken together and running over... God will cause men to give unto your bosom."

Day 180 — June 28

THE FEAR OF death is a tormentor to those who do not know the Lord. When we know our Father in heaven, and we know where we're going after we die... The thought of death can actually seem pleasant... I plan to enjoy every single minute of this life that God has given me, but better yet... The best is yet to come... "Oh death, where is your sting?"

EXAMPLE IS NOT just a good way to teach, it is the absolute best way to teach, and many times it is the only way to teach. Talk is cheap when we are not honoring what we say. The old adage that says, "Do as I say, not as I do," is arrogant and unfair, and it teaches others that it's OK to cheat, and violate your own core values. God's word is pretty clear on this issue; he says "you will know them by their works." It's not so much what you are saying, but what you are doing, that tells the tale.

Day 181 — June 29

WE ALL KNOW that person that you can't teach, or help because they do everything their own way... If you try to share with them...they have been there and done that... The word says "a wise man will hear, and will increase learning; and a man of understanding will attain wise counsel." Always stay open, and teachable... there is nothing more pitiful than an old stubborn person who thinks they know it all.

GOD TELLS US to "live quietly and mind our own affairs" and I think that is a nice way of telling us to mind our own business. This does not mean that you don't try to help people, but many times people really don't want your help, and this is what God meant when he said "don't throw your pearls to swine." It is the right thing to offer a hand, but learn when you're wasting your time, and move on to those who are ready to receive.

Day 182 — June 30

OVER 2000 BIBLICAL prophetic words have come to pass on the earth...and even today many more are in the process of fulfillment...The Bible is still the best-selling book in the world, because it has proven to be the absolute truth...It is filled with history, truth, prophecy, over 6,000 invaluable promises and God's wisdom, and those who read it will have a "light upon your path." And remember that "hearing the word of God is healing to all your flesh."

"KNOW THEREFORE THAT the LORD your God is God, the faithful God who keeps covenant and steadfast love with those who love Him and keep His commandments, to a thousand generations" our God is so faithful and trustworthy... Men will let you down, but God will always be there for you. "Draw close to him and he will draw close to you."

IT IS A privilege to write this foreword for a woman who has been such a profound blessing in my life. My mother-in-law is a shining example of grace, wisdom, and unwavering faith. She has not only been a loving support to me but also a steadfast role model—one who embodies what it means to live with purpose, generosity, and devotion to God.

Her life is a testament to using one's gifts for good. Whether through her words, her actions, or the simple yet powerful act of listening, she pours into the lives of those around her. She offers guidance with wisdom, encouragement with love, and prayer with sincerity. In a world that can often feel hurried and disconnected, she remains a steady source of comfort and inspiration, always ready to lift others up. This book is a reflection of who she is—a woman of faith, strength, and deep compassion. I have no doubt that the words within these pages will encourage and inspire you, just as she has done for so many. It is my hope that as you read, you will be touched by the same wisdom, love, and faithfulness that she so effortlessly shares with the world.

– With love, **Michelle Solis, Daughter in law**

 # July

Day 183 July 1

WHAT SCARES YOU? For me it is earthquakes, snakes, and hell…We in this life take hell lightly…but hell is very real, and we should all quiver at the very thought of it…There are only 2 afterlife destinations available, and both give the chance to choose…But if you choose not to choose, you will default to hell! You cannot default to heaven…You must choose! Your only ticket to heaven is Jesus…Choose wisely.

ALWAYS DO WHAT is right and you will never have to feel guilty. Guilt comes when you are not honoring your core values. No matter what happens in your life, if you have made good, Godly choices and treated people with respect, guilt has no place in your life. Guilt is a tormentor and will cause you to do things you should not do and cause you to make choices that you should not make. Make restitution when possible, ask God for forgiveness, and shake it off.

Day 184 — July 2

EVERYONE LOVES THE sensational, and when you focus on the scriptures, you will see the spectacular every single day... The word says "The devil has blinded the minds of those who do not believe, they cannot see the light of the good news." They are blinded to the things of God...Life through a secular lens is so dull compared to the brilliance of a person who focuses on scripture.

WHEN PEOPLE DO harm to others, pray that God repay them. "Vengeance belongs to God" not you...Do not try to take vengeance, however, you do need to be aware of those around you who may intend to do you harm. "Be wise as a serpent and gentle as a dove." God will handle your offender if you will truly give it to him. "God will make good what was meant for evil" when you trust him.

Day 185　　　　　　　　　　　　July 3

GREATNESS IN ONE word is service…"Those who are to be great in the kingdom of God, must first become servant to all." The simplest act of service can change a life…Spend your days helping others in whatever way you find…Life is empty and vain without service to others…And, "Whatever good thing you do for others, God will do for you."

LIFE IS TROUBLED and filled with physical limitations, but remember "What is impossible with man is possible with God." Obstacles are a breeze for God, and he uses your weaknesses and your limitations to work towards good for you. "In your weakness, God is made strong." The weaker you are, the stronger God will be in your life. "God's grace is sufficient for you."

Day 186   July 4

USE YOUR PERSONAL influence to encourage and help others…There are people who you are uniquely capable of using your influence to change their life. Be cognizant of what influence or income you have within your sphere of influence to help others. "Whatever good thing you do for others, God will do for you."

SECRETS ARE OFTEN rooted in pride or shame. It is actually healthy to share. This does not mean that you should blab everything to everyone, but sharing with trusted people, and asking them to pray is vital. When we put light on a dark subject, it is very healing. "Walk by the light of the day so we don't stumble."

Day 187   July 5

THERE IS POWER in the hardships of life…Do not curl up in a ball, but rather do what you know to do and "God will give you the strength sufficient for the day." Every single trial that you go through in life is adding to your ability to not only help others, but to help yourself through the other trials that are most certainly ahead…The old adage that says "the iron that has been through the fire is the strongest" is absolutely true. You got this 😺

YOUR TESTIMONY IS your most powerful message. Share your testimony. Share about your life before you knew Jesus. Share how you came to the Lord and then share how your life has changed. Be transparent about your problems and the things that God has done to correct them. Don't let shame or pride prevent you from giving a testimony. We overcome the enemy by the blood of the Lamb, and the word of our testimony."

Day 188 — July 6

"SIN DOES NOT always include doing something wrong…It can be a sin of omission…If we see something wrong and do nothing…This is a sin! Sins of omission are rampant in our country as we sit back and ignore what is being done to our children as they confuse them about their sexuality… "It is better to have a millstone tied around your neck and thrown into the deepest part of the ocean than to harm one of these little ones." Apathy is sin!"

THERE'S A FINE line between gossip and being an honest, open person. When we speak of gossip, it usually has to do with the intent of the heart. There are those who live their life in secret. This need for privacy can come from many different reasons, and we need to respect their needs. Then there are those, such as myself, who don't even close their blinds at night because they live so openly. Be sensitive to the needs of others, and always look at a person's heart before you judge them. "Consider others more important than yourself."

Day 189   July 7

IT IS NOT God›s will that men should suffer...He created a perfect world and he "made man upright, but man has devised many schemes" and unfortunately, those schemes have caused much havoc on our planet...It is the choices of men and many times we are victims to their choices. Keep your eyes on God as you navigate through the landmines of life... He promises that "he will put a light on your path."

THERE ARE SOME things that will only be changed by a move of God, and prayer can bring God on the scene to make that change, and corporate prayer is even more powerful. Don't hide things that need agreement in prayer. When we keep things in the dark, they only get bigger and more worrisome. Share with a trusted, caring friend or even a prayer group. "A three-braided cord is hard to break."

Day 190   July 8

SOME PRAYERS ARE answered at once and others take time and even years...This is usually because there is a process involved in the answer to your prayer...Then there is also the mystery of unanswered prayers...Sometimes God does not answer prayer because your request may not be good for you, or he may have something better for you. "You have not because you ask not" "Pray and do not faint." Ask and then believe that God has your best interest at heart...

"WHEN YOU PRAY, give thanks and ask God for help. It is completely appropriate to pray for yourself. I find myself mumbling little prayers all day long, whether it be for a parking space, direction, safety, even to help me find missing things... I have learned to pray about everything, and even though God says, "I know your needs even before you ask." He still tells us "We have not because we ask not" ASK!!"

Day 191   July 9

JOHN WESLEY ONCE said "God does nothing in the world except by prayer" I believe these words are true, with the exception of the providential work of God...Prayer was established by God and I have heard people ask: Why do we need to pray? Doesn't God know what needs to be done? I guess we could say that is one of the mysteries about God...All we know is we have to do what he says. "Ask and you shall receive, Seek and you shall find, Knock and the door shall be opened." "Pray without ceasing"

DO YOU EVER wonder why God is holding back vengeance on the world? It is because of us Christians. Just as he did not destroy Sodom and Gomorrah until he got Lot and his family out...he is holding back because of the church! As the world is turning against Christianity, they don't realize we are the very thing that is protecting them from God's vengeance. "If I find 50 righteous people in the city of Sodom and Gomorrah, I will spare the whole place for their sake." and in the end, he spared it for one righteous family!! Thank you Jesus.

Day 192 — July 10

THERE IS A progression of prayer...Prayer is a desire or a wish...Fervent prayer is a sense of lack or desperation...intercessory prayer is to fall in with, or sacrifice your own needs as you pray...Ask, seek and knock...are all continuous action.... Sometimes we desire so we ask...Or we have a burden so we seek...And then in desperation we knock and never quit, even to the point of pounding on the door... "Pray and do not faint" a desperate kind of prayer will be heard and answered. "Pray without ceasing." Pray until something happens.

THERE IS SUCH a clashing of cultures in our times. There is no longer a gray area...everything is black or white and God says, "If you are lukewarm, I will spew you out of my mouth." We cannot straddle a fence or participate in apathy...we must take a side. Good or evil, black or white, truth or lies. "I lay before you life and death, blessing and cursing...Choose life"

Day 193

July 11

HAVE YOU EVER asked God for something and He didn't answer? And then later you realized that what you asked for was not what you really wanted... And you actually say, "Thank God He didn't answer that prayer." I believe this is true of every unanswered prayer... God knows what is best for us. "God knows your needs even before you ask." Yet He still tells us, "You have not because you ask not..." Always ask anyway, and trust that it will be God's will, not yours.

"GOD HAS A plan for your life," and it is found in prayer. When you are prompted by God to do something, even if it seems weird... do it anyway, because powerful things happen when you follow God's direction. The ripple effect of your day while following your mission will last for eternity.

Day 194 — July 12

"BLESSED ARE THOSE who have never seen and yet still believe." A blessing falls on all believers just for believing. Signs and wonders are wonderful... But it is immature and actually a weak faith that needs a sign or wonder to believe... "Only believe."

"IF YOU SOW to the flesh, you are going to reap destruction." And if you touch the children, you're going to bring a certain judgment that God will not tolerate. Woke will go broke!! Steer clear of all of this evil stuff that is permeating our country, because God is going to rise up and change things. Be prepared!

Day 195   July 13

WHAT WE OBTAIN too cheaply we perceive too lightly... What is it about men that makes them think it must be better if it costs more? When we have skin in the game, we are always more involved and aware... and yet, the best things in life are usually free... Especially our salvation... Jesus paid it all on the cross... "In everything give thanks."

A GRAB FOR power will always end badly. You have to earn leadership before it will be rewarded by God. Not everyone is called to be a leader, and leadership is not the only noble position... There is no friendship or organization that doesn't need a loyal, dedicated follower. Be who God called you to be, and "run your race as if to win."

Day 196   July 14

"ALL THINGS WORK together for good, for those who believe and love God and are called according to God's purpose for them." And this, folks, is what we are seeing with the attempted assassination of Donald Trump. We pray for those who were in harm's way and even lost a life… But we thank God that the prayers we have prayed to surround Donald Trump have protected him in this time, and I assure you, it will work toward good, just as promised… In Jesus' name, Amen.

"FAN THE FLAME and stir up the passion that is within you." I watch those who find the things of God and life in general boring… and my take on that is, if you're bored with life, you are the one who is boring… Choose to encourage yourself and don't wait for others to do it for you. When you encourage yourself, you will find that it has a ripple effect that will encourage and bring joy to others.

Day 197 — July 15

MANY PEOPLE ARE hardhearted because they have been trampled on in life… They put up walls of defense to protect themselves… "It is God's loving kindness working through you that draws others to repentance." Be kind because you never know when your words can break through and actually save a life.

ASK GOD TO frustrate the plan of the enemy, to dry up their funds, to humiliate them, and bind their evil works in the name of Jesus. Remember that "what is bound on earth is bound in heaven." Your words have power. And there is nothing wrong with this kind of prayer. In fact, I believe it is our duty to speak this out. This is what God meant when He told us to "speak to the mountain and tell it to be removed"—mountains, or problems of any kind.

Day 198 — July 16

BE CAREFUL WHO your role models are... It is said there are five people in your life who will impact who you will become... "Be not deceived, bad company corrupts good behavior." This can even include family members... Guard yourself as you protect your character from those bad examples... Be positive when you are forced to be around negativity... Do not give in to their ways, but make every effort to help them make positive corrections in their own character by setting a good example...

WHEN YOU ARE asking God for something important, go the extra mile when asking. Never give up your plea. Take your limitations to God and plead for His mercy and grace to fall on you. Fast, intercede, get agreements in prayer, put on sackcloth if need be. But get God's attention as you "push through the crowd to touch the hem of His garment."

Day 199 — July 17

"NEVER DESPISE SMALL beginnings." I thoroughly believe that small beginnings are important... You grow with your start... There is also a scripture that says, "Quickly gotten, quickly lost." That slow, steady growth is very important to your future success... Don't grumble about it and don't despise it... And don't think that you can't start something because you have to start so small... Just do it... And then walk it out...

PEOPLE OF FAITH have a deeper understanding of evil and good. We often ask, "Are they blind or what?" And the answer is, yes, they are blind. "The god of this age has blinded the eyes of the unbelievers." When someone cannot see the light, it is doubtful that they are saved. "Having eyes, they do not see, and having ears, they do not hear." But He gives understanding to believers. Don't be surprised when unbelievers don't get it. They really are blind. Pray for them.

Day 200 — July 18

BE PROACTIVE AS you prepare your heart by reading and studying the Word... When the Word is heard even once, it never dies... It is a seed that gets planted in the human heart and will eventually grow and produce a harvest... "The Word never comes back void." "The gospel seed will always accomplish what it is sent out to do."

FEAR NOT THOSE things that will undoubtedly come upon you. "In this world, you will have trouble." But always remember that God promises to walk through troubles with you. Anything you go through is for a limited amount of time. Be encouraged. "This too shall pass." God knows your trial, and with every trial comes a lesson of growth... In the mud and scum of things, something always sings. "Be faithful unto death." God preserves the faithful.

Day 201 — July 19

WHEN YOUR LIFE is crowded with too many things, it will choke out the pursuit of God... These are thorns that choke out the good things in life... "What profit is it to receive the whole world and lose your soul?" Weed out your life and keep your priorities in order... Faith, family, friends, fitness, and finances... in that order. "Search me, God, and know my heart. Test me and know my anxious thoughts... See if there is any offensive way in me and lead me in the way of truth."

WE HAVE TO overcome our fears and step out of our box. We tend to do things repetitively like our parents did them, and many times we refuse to change. Although there is something special in tradition, there are changes that need to be made. Growth is imperative. Evaluate your family traditions and make sure they are still worth passing down. Weed out. "Behold, I make all things new."

Day 202 — July 20

DRY SEASONS IN our life cause us to grow deeper and stronger roots... Just as a dry climate causes trees to grow deep roots to get water... Shallow roots will topple over in a storm, while deep roots can withstand all sorts of storms... Those who have endured trials and come out victorious will always be the strongest... "After you have suffered for a little while, God Himself will restore you and make you strong, firm, and steadfast."

WHAT DO WE do when someone offends us? We forgive them and choose to love above all else. We all sinned against Jesus, and He forgave us and gave His life for us anyway. Cover over the sin with love. Love through the offenses of others. This is called mercy, and you can never go wrong with mercy. "Those who show mercy will have mercy shown to them."

Day 203   July 21

WHEN WE HAVE been forged by fire, we are stronger, smarter, and just more able all around... "The iron that has been through the fire is the strongest." Those who have gone through trials are the ones who others can count on for wise counsel... "Count it all joy when you go through the fiery trials because it is perfecting you..."

YOU WILL NEVER receive a miracle if you sit around whining and feeling sorry for yourself... Rise up and confess out loud: "Sorrow may happen for the night, but joy will come in the morning!" Walk it out, believe God's word, and trust in Him, and you will see restoration. "Has He not said it and will He not do it?"

Day 204   July 22

WE ARE TOLD in the scriptures to have "The God kind of faith"... Then He goes on to tell us that this kind of faith is: "You must believe it in your heart, confess it with your mouth, and you will have whatsoever you say." This kind of faith can move a mountain... It can believe for miracles, and it can heal the sick... Ask God to give you the God kind of faith and remember that "faith comes by hearing the word of God," so read the Bible!

YOUR MISTAKES AND your failures are not final. God will never define you by your mistakes. Every man and woman on planet Earth has messed up at one time or another... The main thing is that you pick yourself up and get back in the race... Your mistakes and your failures are an extra bite out of the apple, because you have learned something that others haven't... "There is, therefore, no condemnation to those who are in Christ Jesus."

Day 205 — July 23

"GOD'S WORD SPOKE everything into being… He gave us the same kind of power. He told us that He was leaving the power to us, and if we really believe, we can "speak to the mountain and tell it to be removed," and it has to go… We can "lay hands on the sick and they will recover." We can "ask anything in His name and He will do it." And the only caveat is that we "Only Believe." WOW!"

"A FOOL VENTS all his feelings, but a wise man holds them back." Feelings are fickle from one minute to the next. The wise man learns to control his feelings and to zip his lip. Harsh words spoken in a moment of bad feelings can destroy relationships. Be slow to speak as you analyze the situation. This can save so many problems. And remember that "gentle words are like apples of gold set in frames of silver." Almost any problem can be solved with gentle words.

Day 206   July 24

FORGIVE AND FORGET... I don't think so! We can choose to forgive, but forgetting is difficult... Forgiveness does not mean that you do not remember... To remember is normal, and it can be used to protect yourself and minister to others... Remembering is not bad, but it must not be used to hold unforgiveness. "As you forgive others, God will forgive you." Forgiveness defined means: to release or send away...

AS CHRISTIANS, WE are living on the edge of two worlds that clash. We must live in the world, but it is not our home, and our values are at total odds with the world. America had been pretty easy in the past, but the clashing of the two kingdoms has been intensified. We live in a satanic stronghold where the devil dwells. But always remember that our God is the true ruler. Hang on, and "be strong and courageous." "What is impossible for man is possible for God." Hold fast to the name of Jesus, because in the end... We win!!!

Day 207 — July 25

"WHEN YOU HOLD unforgiveness, God does not hear your prayers." If you have ever wondered why a prayer was not answered... Check your heart... Unforgiveness holds a high price... It is like shooting yourself in the foot... When God says something, He means it... "Has He not said it, and will He not do it?" When you hold anger against someone, it is like drinking acid and expecting the other person to die... Anger and unforgiveness are pure poison to the flesh...

SOMETIMES WHAT BRINGS victory is simply holding on to what you know to be right. It isn't always about knowing a bunch of stuff, but simply doing what you know to do. You do not have to have special skills; you just need to trust God and hold on. "When you have done all you know to do, stand and believe."

Day 208 — July 26

"WHERE YOUR TREASURE is, there will your heart be also." A generous heart is linked with abundant faith... When your faith is big, you never worry about being generous because you know that God will replace anything you choose to give to others... "With whatever measure you use to give, it will be measured back to you"— spoonfuls, shovels, buckets, or truckloads? Your choice.

OUR CULTURE REQUIRES that we tolerate everything, or we are called racist, homophobic, white supremacist, white privileged, prejudiced, and more. And yet, there is no tolerance required for our Christian values. "Good is called evil, and evil is called good." God's word is counted as judgmental. But be assured, the ways of God lead to joy, peace, good health, and true happiness. "One day, every knee shall bow." Stay connected.

Day 209 July 27

REWARDS FROM GOD are real, and when you serve God in this life, you can expect to be rewarded for your service... To serve God means to honor Him and love others. Although these works will not get us to heaven, they will bring great rewards in this life. "Delight yourself in the Lord, and He will give you the desires of your heart."

"THE FEAR OF man brings a snare, but whoever trusts in the Lord shall be safe." We are living in troubling times... There are many people out there trying to hurt others and take what they have. This is the time to put your faith in God... We do need to be cautious, but we should never walk in fear. "Be wise as a serpent and gentle as a dove."

Day 210   July 28

GOD NEVER USES fear, guilt, or torment. But we can choose to do things that bring about fear, guilt, and torment, and this is because God gives us the right to choose... "I lay before you life and death, blessing and cursing. Choose life." "Fear not" is in the Bible 365 times—one for every day of the year... Do not allow fear, guilt, or torment to trump God's command...

"THOUGH YOU MAY weep for a night, joy will come in the morning." When you go through sorrow, always remember that God will restore whatever is lost, and there will be a time of joy. This time will pass, so don't react or do anything foolish because "joy will come in the morning." Life is filled with ups and downs... When you find yourself in one of the downs, keep looking forward because the up is right around the corner.

Day 211 — July 29

WHAT YOU DWELL on is what you will manifest in your life... Have a positive perspective about your past because it has brought you to all the good things in your life today... Your broken road has brought you your family, your friends, your mate, and every sweet thing in your life. Be of good cheer and "Run your race with endurance."

THERE ARE TIMES in all of our lives when we feel so stretched that we can't go another step. But in these times, if we trust God, He will strengthen our ability to go farther. "He gives us the strength sufficient for the day." Remind Him of that precious promise when you feel stretched beyond your ability... And remember, "In your weakness, He is made strong."

Day 212 — July 30

WE ALL LOVE loopholes, but there are no loopholes when it comes to "loving God" and "loving your neighbor." These two commands encompass our whole charge as children of God... Loopholes are legal, and it is fun to watch for some and even jump through a few... But never try to shortchange the love of God or the love of your neighbor...

BURNOUT HAPPENS WHEN we are doing things, but they are not done with love. It is exhausting to work tediously at something that is not done in love. "Do all things as unto the Lord." If your job requires that you do something you don't enjoy, try switching to an attitude of doing it "as unto the Lord." Burnout is not good for you or anyone else. Take the time to get the break you need.

Day 213   July 31

MANY PEOPLE HAVE had a bad start... But "Never despise small beginnings" ... Every single person has the opportunity to better themselves! Never just accept that you were born there and have to stay there... Get out of there!! Become all you want to be and all that God created you to be. We are blessed to live in a country where everyone has opportunity... It may take some hard work... And remember, "God blesses the work of your hands" ... Get busy and make it happen...

A MISSION IN your life will keep you young and strong. An adventure to seek, a wrong to make right, or someone to rescue... all of these things are a fountain of youth. It does not matter how old you are or what your physical condition is, there is always someone or something that can use your help. "God blesses the work of your hands." Keep your hands moving all the days of your life.

My Jack is so creative and fun ...
And if you're looking for a variety of conversation, he is the one ...
He never forgets his Bubby and we always have lots to share,
When it comes to grandsons, I know he truly cares...
As a child, he was smart as a whip
Always delighting us with his intellectual quips...
And when it came to trivia, he would outdo the best,
He knew a little about everything and would adlib the rest...
At sports he outdid everything he tried,
and his comedian acts made us laugh till we cried...
He always wakes up happy and goes to bed with a smile!
As he juggles life's problems all of the while...
There's no doubt about it, he's headed for success,
Wherever he sets his hand, he beats all the rest...
His very best trait is, he trusts God with all of his heart,
And God's favor upon him sets him apart...
Blessings upon him as he begins his adult life,
With prosperity in everything and barren of strife...
I love this young grandson more than words can say, and for his
   success I sincerely pray...

– Velma Hagar for Jack Solis Grandson

 # August

Day 214 — August 1

THERE IS A limit to how much a person can take... I think all of us can get to a point of desperation, where we have just had enough... Jesus tells us "To turn the other cheek"... He also said that there should not be a limit to forgiveness... When you choose not to forgive others, God will not forgive you... This will leave you wide open to the horrors of a life without God... Forgive... and "Pray for those who have mistreated you"... and then keep your distance from them... "We are called to a life of peace."

"IF WE JUDGE ourselves, we will not be judged." Take the time often to evaluate yourself and ask God to "create in me a clean heart." Don't beat yourself up for wrongs that you know you have done... Once you've asked God to forgive you, "He doesn't even remember your sin anymore." "God is faithful to finish the work He has started in you." Do your part, and He will do His.

Day 215   August 2

SPEAK KIND WORDS... Words are so valuable... They have the ability to lift people up, and they also have the ability to destroy... "The power of life and death is in the tongue." Be careful how you wield this powerful little tool that has the ability to give life or "set your life on a course of destruction."

THE RACE IS not always given to the swiftest or the strongest, but to the one who endures. I can›t stress it enough that if you quit, you are never going to win. I honestly believe that the hardest fight of any project is right at the end when we are tempted to grow weary, but God›s word clearly says, «Grow not weary of well-doing because in due season you shall have your reward.» There is a due season when everything will come to fruition, our part is to stand in there and believe right to the end.

Day 216   August 3

"FAITH WITHOUT WORKS is dead." If you believe that we should do nothing but pray... You are missing the boat! If your church feels that you should never be active in the things of the world to make things better... You need to change churches... Yes, prayer is powerful... But without works, things will not happen. Pray, and then get busy and do something as "God directs your steps."

THERE IS NOTHING that will disqualify a person from being accepted and saved by Jesus. Many followers of Jesus have a tainted past. "God wishes that all men would be saved." Walk with God and let Him heal your heart of all the hurts and pains of your past. Jesus sees in you what the world cannot see, and He will bring out the best in you, as He "finishes the work He has started in you."

Day 217 — August 4

WHEN YOU PRAY for other people, God will not override the other person's will in order to answer your prayer. This does not mean that your prayer doesn't work... It means that it may take time for God to convict their hearts... They still have the choice, and they may even act worse while you are praying for them... But keep praying and remember "The effectual fervent prayers of a righteous man avails much."

"DELIGHT YOURSELF IN the Lord, and He will give you the desires of your heart." So the formula is: Desire, Diligence, Delight. First comes the desire for something, and then comes the works that must go into the desire that will cause the delight to happen. I love this promise! Remember that all of God's promises are true... But there is a caveat attached to each promise... Do your part, and God will do His.

Day 218   August 5

WHEN YOU ARE waiting for something that you have prayed for, it may seem like nothing is happening because there is so little outward progress... But after you reach your goal, and you look back, you will notice that there was progress as you went along... When you recognize these little advances... Stop and do a partial celebration... Think about how far you have come rather than how far you have to go... "God is faithful to finish the work He has started."

PRAYERS OF DESPERATION, prayers under compulsion, that are specific and prayed with confidence in God are so powerful, and when we pray with an intense sincerity for others, God esteems us. "You have not because you ask not." Glorify God before prayer and remind Him of things He has done, and the things He has done for others because "what He has done for one, He will do for another."

Day 219 — August 6

HOW DO YOU know when God is calling you to do something? First, you will have a passion for it, and it will always be on your mind... You will be willing to sacrifice anything to get it... And when it is God, He will give you the faith you need to get the job done, no matter how long it takes... Just take the first step toward it, and God will direct... "God works in us to will and to do His good pleasure."

"I WILL GIVE you the treasures of darkness and hidden riches in secret places, that you may know that I am the Lord." When was the last time that you asked God to show you a secret, hidden treasure? I have always loved the mystery of this beautiful promise... so much so that I named my book after it. Join me today as we ask God to show us a hidden treasure in a secret place.

Day 220   August 7

REMEMBER THAT IN the midst of your struggle, you are still loved by God... There is nothing you can do that will stop God from loving you... But there are still consequences for the things that you choose that go against His word... Just as a loving father in the flesh would not let his precious child get away with doing things that would harm him... So, it is with our Father in heaven. "God chastens those He loves."

YOU CAN KNOW the direction you are to go when you spend time every day praying and seeking God. When in doubt, ask God to direct you. "Lean not on your own understanding, but in all things trust God, and He will make your paths straight." Make your plans but leave room for God to make adjustments.

Day 221 — August 8

THE STRUGGLE IS hard, but the success of the God-given vision is worth it... Sometimes we even move away from the vision because the struggle is so intense, and sometimes the vision is for a later appointed time... God promises us that "He has a plan for our life and it's a good plan"... Stay on target, as you walk out the details... Remember that if it is God's plan for you, He will enable you to complete it.

BE A PERSON who picks people up. There are many reasons why people need to be picked up, whether it be physically, financially, or emotionally. Be that person who is sensitive to the needs of others and is willing to do what is within your ability to help. When you choose to help others, God will help you. "Whatever good thing one man does for another, God will do for him."

Day 222 — August 9

THE THINGS THAT hurt us in life are not always what we do, but it can also be what we allow. "A little leaven leavens the whole batch." Allowing wrong things in your life in any area is opening the door to pain and danger. You cannot compromise your life or you will ruin your good life. Keep your surroundings tidy... and this can include keeping a distance from some people who bring chaos. "We are called to a life of peace."

SO MANY PEOPLE take this scripture lightly... They imply that all sin is the same... And yet God calls this particular sin out and says it is better to have a millstone tied around their neck and thrown into the deepest part of the ocean than to harm the little children... Leave our children alone!

Day 223 — August 10

WHATEVER YOU FOCUS on has a cost... Spend your days focusing on the things of God... Your focus is valuable because where you put your focus is where you will go... Keep your eye on the prize and send your heart first and your body will follow... "Set your mind on the things above, not on the things of earth..."

INTEGRITY MEANS THAT every area of your life has to harmonize with what is right, it means complete adherence to moral and ethical principles. You cannot compartmentalize your life. It must be all-encompassing. "He who is unfaithful in little things will also be unfaithful in big things." To be thought of as a faithful and ethical person is one of the nicest compliments anyone could pay you.

Day 224   August 11

IT IS GOOD for us to struggle because somewhere in that struggle, God will set us up to see things that we would never have seen... Struggles are lessons... Do not waste time whining about what's going on... Instead, pay attention to what you have learned... The sooner we learn the lesson, the sooner the trial is finished... "Count it all joy when you're going through the fiery trials because it is perfecting you."

THERE COMES A time in life when we need to realize that the things wrong with us are not about what our mommy and daddy did to us when we were little... but rather it is about the choices that we have made. Make a choice that whatever happened to you will become a testimony and will be used to help others. With God in your life, this is totally and completely possible! "Forgetting those things that are behind and moving towards those things that are ahead." Get over it!!

Day 225   August 12

ALL OF US HAVE experienced that person who just always seems to be divisive and argumentative... This is what the Bible says about them; "Reject a divisive man after the first and second admonition, knowing that such a person is warped and sinning, being self-condemned." When these people try to pick a fight with you, and especially on social media... Do not enter in... Respectfully block them or walk away... "With whatever is within you... Be at peace with all men."

YOU CANNOT MIX sin in with your Godly Walk. "Darkness cannot be where there is light." You may get by with wavering back and forth for a short time, but eventually, it will come crashing down on you. "I lay before you life and death, blessing and cursing... choose life." It's all about choices, folk.

Day 226   August 13

OBEDIENCE HAS TO do with our outward actions, while submission has to do with the inward heart... God looks at the heart, and judges accordingly... While we tend to look at the outside... God only sees the heart... "The issues of life flow from the heart." Always check your heart to be sure your motives are in line...

JESUS MINISTRY WAS to do good and heal the sick. And He said that "My church will do the same works and even greater works." We have a mandate to continue that anointing. We are called to operate like Jesus. If you see someone in need... Take the time to pray for them, and lay hands on the sick. "If a believer lays hands on the sick, they shall recover." What a great promise...

Day 227 — August 14

THE SPIRITUAL REALM is very real, and it has a great impact on the physical world... Just because you cannot see it with your eyes does not mean things do not exist... Some things can only be fought in the spirit through prayer... "We wrestle not against flesh and blood, but against powers, principalities, and the rulers of darkness..."

DO NOT ALLOW people to hold you down. If you have been gifted with a gift of enthusiasm, live it out. Many will be offended by exuberance, and that offense is fed mostly by envy. The word enthusiasm means "with God." Never curb this amazing gift. "Do everything as unto the Lord." Never tone down your passion.

Day 228   August 15

"WHEN YOU ARE waiting on God, don't just stand around and do nothing... Get busy and help someone else. Keep yourself moving. God's word says "God directs the steps of the righteous." This is indicative of action or movement... So keep your hands and your feet moving and God will direct... "In due season you shall have your reward."

WHERE YOU CHOOSE to go, others will follow. Your choices can have eternal effects on those around you. Choices are serious. We can actually change the direction of thousands of people throughout our lifetime. It is said that the average person can affect up to 10,000 people in a lifetime. Set an example to all who meet you. Acknowledge God in the rough waters and "He will direct your path."

Day 229   August 16

POWER GOES WHERE your attention flows... Don't pay attention to things that aggravate you... It is a waste of energy! Ignore people who are saying ignorant, divisive, rude, or mean things... "Set your mind on the things above and not on the things below." Keep your attention on those things that are productive and that you want in your life, because those are the things that your attention will manifest...

THE BIGGEST DIVERSIONS in life that will take you off your God-given path are usually something fun and exciting. Be careful not to allow anything to pull you off your God-given course. There are specific things in your life that only you have been called to carry out. Keep your eyes on the road ahead as you fulfill your calling. "God has a good plan for your life, a plan to prosper you and not harm you."

Day 230 — August 17

HUMILITY AND MEEKNESS is power under control... God's word says, "the meek shall inherit the Earth"... Meek, defined, means: Quiet, gentle, courteous, and submissive... But a less known definition is: Channeling one's strengths to serve God, while having the power to do something, but choosing not to for someone else's benefit. Basically, meek means "kind."

HONESTY AND TRUTH make you strong. When you are honest and transparent, there is something so liberating about it. Do not hide things in the darkness or stand behind a façade. Remember that the darkness causes ugly things to grow, while the light expels the darkness. "Walk in the light, and you will not stumble."

Day 231   August 18

THINGS WILL NEVER change unless you change... It is said that insanity is to keep doing the same things over and over and expecting things to be different... Nothing will change, until you change... Evaluate your life and Ask God to help you make positive changes, and to "finish the work that he has started in you" ..." God has a plan for your life and it's a good plan... A plan to prosper you and not to harm you. "But you have to let him make the changes.

I BELIEVE IN the right to choose! And so does God... He tells us "I lay before you, life and death, blessing, and cursing... Choose life" God allows you to choose death if you want, and we have no right to stop anyone from choosing whatever they want...but the consequences can be so great when you don't choose life. God will forgive you for every bad choice you ever make... But the consequences of those bad choices belong to you.

Day 232   August 19

GOD HEARS YOUR silent prayers…He knows your heart, even though he says, "You have not because you ask not" … While it is important to ask, God knows your heart and in times of deep sorrow or pain…God can hear the silent scream of a wounded heart, and he says that "He will never break a bruised reed."

MANY PEOPLE FEEL like they are stuck, and they don't know which way to go. If you trust God and you ask him for direction, he will open a door for you. Don't be afraid to walk through it… I am convinced that we have missed so many blessings in our life because we were afraid to take a chance on something new. Once you have acknowledged God… Make the move and take the chance. "He promises to direct your steps."

Day 233 — August 20

GRIEF IS PART of life...God says: "there is a time for everything under the sun" and this includes "A time to mourn and a time to dance" But grief can be so painful if it is not a clean and gentle grief...Bitterness, anger, and guilt will make grief way more painful... Never allow these three tormentors to enter into your grief...A gentle and clean grief includes sweet memories, smiles, regrets. (not guilt) Lots of tears... as well as a deep faith that you will see them again.

THE WORLD IS full of mean-spirited people, and we are called to pray for them. It is not always easy to pray for someone that you would like to see lightning come down and strike 😊 But always remember that God loves everybody, he knows their heart, he knows the pain they are feeling, he knows what causes them to be mean-spirited, and he wants them saved!! Our job is to simply pray for them. It is God's battle, not ours.

Day 234 — August 21

THE CONSEQUENCE OF the sins of others affects all of us. The evil and chaos we see in the world is the result of not obeying God's principles...Many of us are victims of the choices of those around us... Hang on to God's promises as we navigate through these troubled times... One of my favorites that I remind God of often is "You will only see the reward of the wicked with your eyes, but it will not come near you." Find the promises in the Bible, because I assure you, we are going to need them! They are your inheritance... And you must know where they are to claim them.

LIFE IS FILLED with ups and downs... But as long as you keep God in the center and lean on him in the down times, you will come out victorious. I can't even begin to tell you what a difference it is for me these days when there is a down time, compared to how I used to be before I learned to trust the Lord. "He promises us a peace that goes beyond understanding" even in the middle of disaster. My prayer is that every person reading this will find that peace, by making Jesus the Lord of their life...

Day 235 — August 22

"FAVOR SURROUNDS ME LIKE A SHIELD!" This is one of those wonderful promises that we need to claim every day...When you have God's favor on your life, you have everything you need to be successful, happy, and a beautiful human being in every area of life... His favor will fall on those that seek to serve him and follow the principles that he has established...

ALWAYS BE ALERT and aware. This is not to mean you are to worry and fret, but we are told "to. Be wise as a serpent and gentle as a dove." "stay alert to the wiles of the enemy." "Watch and pray" there are so many scriptures that imply that we need to wake up! be sober and vigilant because the devil roams around seeking whom he may devour."

Day 236   August 23

DOUBT IS NOT a sin... In fact, it is necessary...Jesus allowed doubting Thomas to check his wound to prove clarity of his uncertainty...As long as you are willing to check the reason for your doubt and accept the outcome of what you have discovered... Never feel guilty about doubt... I love the term that says "trust and verify." Although this term is not scriptural it does confirm scripture..."Out of the mouth of two or three witnesses, a truth becomes established"...

WHEN YOU PRAY God's will, you will always get a positive answer to your prayer. God tells us to "bring me in remembrance of my word." He wants us to remind him of what he said. We need to pay attention to what God tells us to do. If you have a need... Find a promise that fits your need... And remind God of that promise... and that my friends, is how you get prayers answered.

Day 237 — August 24

GOD RAISED UP America for two very specific reasons... Now listen to me closely when I say this, and I do not say it quietly or in fear of offending! I say it boldly and loudly...God raised up America to preach the gospel to the whole world...He prospered us financially so we would have the wherewithal to be able to fulfill that mission...The second, and I believe the most important reason is because he needed a country that would stand with Israel so that he could fulfill his promises for that country...If you choose to vote for anyone who does not fully support Israel...You are voting against everything that the holy Bible stands for...And frankly, you are voting against God..."I will bless those who Bless them and I will curse those who curse them." Your choice.

WE ARE WITNESSING deception and chaos in a way that we've never seen before in our life. But be assured that none of this comes as a surprise to God. If you are a student of the Bible, you realize that every single thing that is happening, has been prophesied in this amazing book that God gave us to follow. 33% of the Bible is prophetic and the majority of those prophecies have either been fulfilled or are in the process of being fulfilled. "There will be signs in the sun, moon, and stars; and on the earth distress of nations, with perplexity, the sea and the waves roaring;" "Now when these things begin to happen, look up and lift up your heads, because your redemption draws near." we are right there folks... I hope you're ready. I am.

Day 238   August 25

WHEN JESUS USES the word "like" it means that this is a parable...A parable represents many different applications, and many times people don't understand even one of the applications... But the more you get to know the Lord, the more the parables will open up to you and become an enormous part of building your life around God's word..." He answered and said unto them, "The mysteries of the Kingdom of Heaven, are given to you, but to them it is not given." God speaks in parables, so that only the people that know him will understand...If you don't understand... Check your heart.

THE BOOK OF revelation should never scare you, but rather encourage you, because it is the uncovering of Jesus. It does include prophetic words as well, but it is basically a great revelation of Jesus, and the blessings related to those who overcome. All the promises in the book of revelation are for those who overcome. So, when you suffer through problems and continue to seek God, you become an overcomer. "To him who overcomes, he will eat from the tree of life." Hang in there and "this too shall pass"

Day 239   August 26

IT IS SAID that the human mind has 80,000 thoughts a day and that 60,000 of those thoughts are repetitive... it is important that we train our mind to stay on positive, productive thoughts, and allow those thoughts to germinate in our life... Always remember that "As a man thinks in his heart, so he is"... be careful what you allow yourself to think about...

"EVERY PATH YOU take leads to a choice, and some of those choices will change the rest of your life. And choices based on ego or pride will almost always take you in the wrong direction. Be very intentional about changes and choices. Just as turning your car in a certain direction will take you to a certain place, the same thing is true with the choices you make along the way. "Acknowledge God in all your ways, and he will direct your path."

Day 240 — August 27

GOD'S WORD SAYS "without a vision people will perish. "You need to have a vision of who you are and where you are going... If you can visualize it... You can do it... you have to have a picture of what God is going to do in your life before it will happen...If you are picturing yourself as a loser and talking smack about yourself, that is right where you're going to go and stay... Get a vision of what you want in your life and then go for it... "As a person believes, so it is."

IF WE CONSISTENTLY do what is right, we will eventually feel right. There is something very satisfying about doing what we know is the right thing to do. Good decisions will change your life! It is definitely easier to make right decisions when things pertain to us...but when we are considering others it can be harder. But remember "whatever good thing one man does for another, God does for them."

Day 241 — August 28

COURAGE TAKES OVER when confidence ends... I don't think any of us are born courageous, and yet God tells us 365 times in the Bible to "Fear Not" ...and we are told to "be strong and courageous." As long as our confidence is intact, we don't need courage because it's very easy to go forward... But "In our weakness, God is made strong" ...So when your confidence has been lost for whatever reason... God can come on the scene, and courage can reign in your life...

JESUS SAID, "IN the end times there would be perilous times." I think we are there. The climate of our times are very serious. It is time to stop being loyal to political parties and pay close attention to who and what we are voting for. Our culture cannot take much more... our history, our traditions, and our morals are being lied about, and changed by a government who seems to be trying to destroy us. Be bold and stand up for what is right.

Day 242 — August 29

WHEN A PERSON rejects God on a continuous basis, the word says that "God will give them over to a depraved mind"... When this happens, they will begin "To see evil as good and good as evil"...I hate to say it, but I think we are seeing this probability becoming a fact in our country...I am amazed at those who do not see evil, and actually support it or call it good...Pray for God to open the blind eyes and to change the hardened hearts...We are spiraling down at an alarming speed... God help us...In Jesus name, Amen...

WE VERY SELDOM need to be reminded of things that we already know, but we all need to be reminded of truths that we may know but are not practicing. God tells us to sing Psalms to one another and remind each other of his goodness. It isn't that we don't know a common verse, but it has power every time it goes out. "The word never comes back void."

Day 243 — August 30

"THE HEART OF a man plans his way, but the Lord directs his steps" ...It is important to have a plan and a vision, but always be open to God redirecting your steps... If you truly acknowledge God and ask him to guide you, he may take you in a whole different direction...Be willing to move in a new direction when you feel that gentle tug, that is peaceful, and has a witness in your own spirit...

WE HAVE A responsibility to stewardship of our time and space and stuff. If you are frivolous with the gifts that God has given you, you will often lose them, and they will be given to someone else who uses good stewardship. "Do not bury your talents" be generous with your gifts, and God will give you increase.

Day 244   August 31

KEEP YOUR MIND clean…Fleshly lusts war against your soul…It isn't just keeping your flesh clean, it is keeping your mind clean as well…Our minds are like a blueprint…What you will allow into your mind will eventually manifest into your natural life…" Whatever things are pure, lovely or beautiful…If there be anything noble, or praiseworthy, think on these things."

YOU HAVE TO make the right choices while you are still hurting. You don't have to feel good before you make good decisions. In fact, I believe it is more important to make good decisions while going through trials. Your choices in the throes of a trial can make all the difference. Always remember that just because your flesh is being tested… Your spirit is still strong and unaffected. Your flesh is weak, but your spirit is strong" "walk in the spirit, and you will not fulfill the lusts of the flesh."

My Erica made me a grandma at a very young age
Ending my youth as I turned the page...
Delighting her Grams with her unique little style,
Learning quite young how to make Grams smile...
We had a Special bond using "Sweet" as our word
While circling our cheek no sassing was heard...
She realized quite young this antic was irresistible
As she cleverly used it to acquire toys by the fistful.
Her Grams was enchanted by this baby girls love
Knowing full well she was a gift from above...
Determined and sure of the path she would take,
Strong willed yet tender as her choices were made...
Successful and smart, entrepreneurial like her dad
Fortune and favor are sure to be had.
Her Grams sends her love straight from her heart
And loves her like crazy as she has from the start.

– Velma Hagar for Erica Solis, Granddaughter

September

Day 245 — September 1

GOD CAN USE the most wretched thing in your life to make you grow... Whatever it is that you have in your life that you wish would be gone is the very thing that God can use to teach you... Unfortunately, we don't learn when things are really good... It usually takes a trial... So learn your lesson well so you can move on... And remember to, "Count it all joy when you go through the fiery trials, because it is perfecting you."

GOD'S WORD SAYS, "The heart of man is deceitful, and who can know it?" God actually warns us to be careful of our own hearts, and this can seem like a contradiction in some ways. But I believe that God is referring to the heart as the center of our being, and we know that, by nature, man is deceitful and wicked without God... A heart becomes tender and productive as it is filled with God's word... "Study to make yourself approved."

Day 246 September 2

EVERYTHING WE DO in life is building our life... Do your best at everything because your work will follow your days... We are all building a house, and we are the sum total of everything we have ever thought, said, or did... What is the foundation you are building on? If you are building on sand... storms in life will destroy your house... while the house built on the rock will withstand all sorts of weather... "Do everything you do as unto the Lord."

WE LEARN NOTIIING from life when we are know-it-alls or think we are right all the time... Choose to listen to others and then evaluate what they have to say... We don't have to always agree with them, but to think that we are above learning from our friends, children, or even our grandchildren is not only ignorant, but it also puts us in a box... "A wise man learns by watching... a fool has to have a rod taken to his back." Always stay open to learning something new.

Day 247 — September 3

THE WORLD AT large looks at your hustle before they see your heart... While God looks at your heart first, the world looks at your outward hustle... Draw others to God by representing Him well with good behavior and a heart that is pure... "Whatever you do, do it all for the glory of God."

JESUS WILLINGLY DIED on the cross to identify with all those who are searching for truth. Are you among them? The word truth in our culture has almost been deemed extinct! You can't believe anything you hear... But I assure you that God's word is still the truth. Walk in it, and you will find the peace that you are seeking. "The word of God is the same yesterday, today, and forever."

Day 248 — September 4

GOD LOVES A true and righteous judgment, and He says, "Woe to judges who judge unrighteously." God's vengeance will fall on the judges who abuse their God-given position... God is omnipotent, but He has turned the earth over to mankind and allows our "choices" to rule... However, there will be a time when God will seize control of the earth and He will destroy all evil... Come, sweet Jesus... 🙏

"THE RACE IS not to the swift, nor the battle to the strong, nor bread to the wise, nor riches to men of understanding, nor favor to men of skill; but time and chance happen to them all." A fear to make a change or take a chance will make the difference between success and failure. I am convinced that those who don't seem to get anywhere also don't make decisions to be proactive. Sometimes there is a small window of time that can change a life. Go for it!!

Day 249   September 5

THE BIBLE HAS proven the test of time... It is over 2,000 years old and is still the number one best-selling book of all time... There are an estimated 100 million copies sold every single year... There are over 6,000 promises in the Bible that have proven true to those who are wise enough to claim them... Jesus fulfilled the 365 prophecies about Himself while He was on Earth... And a huge percentage of other prophecies have been fulfilled or are in the process of being fulfilled... The Bible is an amazing book, and it is sincerely and truly the word of God... "Read the Bible to make yourself approved," and while you're reading it, remember to claim the promise that says, "The word of God is healing to all of the flesh."

THERE IS A security in obedience. If you obey God and are faithful, I guarantee you that God will bless you. "Obedience is better than sacrifice." It doesn't matter what things look like or how long you have been 'at it' without seeing results... If you are obedient, and you are doing things God's way... The doors will open, and the wall will come down... Never give up.

Day 250 September 6

"GIVE GENEROUSLY, FOR your gifts will return to you later." We could never outgive God... The more we give, the more He gives to us... Be generous, not only with your material goods but with your gifts. And remember that "With whatever measure you measure, it will be measured back to you."

WHEN YOU OPERATE in pride, you will block your blessings every time. "Pride comes before destruction, and a haughty spirit before a fall." When you choose to let pride control your life, you are headed for destruction. Always check your motives and be sure you aren't being motivated by pride.

Day 251   September 7

WHEN WE OBEY God, every path that He guides us on is fragrant with His loving kindness and His truth… He tells us to "Acknowledge Him in all our ways and He will make our path straight." Life is full of all sorts of choices, and there are many paths that twist and turn… But the straight path that our Father in Heaven will lay before us is beautiful when we acknowledge Him.

"WHEN GOD OPENS a door, no man can shut it, and when God shuts a door, no man can open it." Stand confident when God has opened a door for you… Push through it and remember that opposition does not mean that God did not open the door… But you have to walk through it. Provision will always be made for God's work, done God's way.

Day 252 — September 8

THERE ARE TIMES that we pray and it seems we wait and wait and do not see an answer. But remember that, like a mustard seed that is put in the ground, it will take time to sprout... And even though we can't see it yet, we trust that it will grow into a huge fruitful tree... Like that tree that cannot be seen yet but is germinating under the ground, is the prayer that has been sent. "There is a time and a season for everything under the sun." "Grow not weary of well-doing, because in due season you shall have your reward."

YOU DO NOT need a lot of strength or wisdom because "In your weakness, God is made strong." But you do need to be faithful and keep God's word. Small faith can move mountains when you put your trust in God. Faithfulness is the whole key. Never give up on God. "I can do all things through Christ who strengthens me."

Day 253 September 9

REVENGE IS NOT sweet... In fact, it can actually make us sick and even kill us... Studies have shown an association between negative emotions, such as anger and revenge, with a variety of destructive physical symptoms, including headaches, depression, backaches, allergic disorders, ulcers, nausea, high blood pressure, and heart attacks... Sadly, while vengeful people plot another's demise, they themselves often develop a painful health problem... Paybacks have a way of paying us back... "Vengeance is mine, says the Lord."

DO WHAT YOU know to do and make decisions... If your decisions are wrong, you can always make changes as you go along... But do not sit and do nothing... Be proactive! In times of uncertainty, move a little slower, and God will direct you. A baby step in the wrong direction can be corrected a lot easier than a large step. Go easy... But go!! "The steps of a righteous man are ordered by the Lord."

Day 254 — September 10

YOU WILL NEVER win if you don't fight... "No weapon formed against you will prosper." "Fight the good fight." What do Christians, who claim they don't want to get involved in things of the world, do with these scriptures? We are all called to be warriors for God... To stand up for the things of God... "To speak for those who cannot speak for themselves"... To protect the innocent, and to even be martyred if necessary for the sake of God's word. "Because you are lukewarm, and neither hot nor cold, I will spit you out of my mouth."

A SHUT DOOR means you are to open another door. Push through. If the project is done right and in line with God, He will open a door. Look for doors to open, and if you are faithful, God will open a door that no one can close. Remain faithful... This is the key to finding the favor of God in your life. "Trust God with all your heart, and He will make your paths straight."

Day 255   September 11

YOU CANNOT JUST confess Jesus as Savior and not take Him as your Lord... Christianity is not a custom-made thing... You cannot have salvation unless you accept His gift of lordship as well... God provides a package deal... You cannot have the banquet without the lordship... "Not everyone who says to Me, 'Lord, Lord,' shall enter the kingdom of heaven, but he who does the will of My Father in heaven."

WHEN YOU GIVE of yourself or your possessions, your gift will keep giving. If you are a fruitful tree to others, you will continuously bear fruit all the days of your life, and as you age, your fruit will even get sweeter. When you serve God by serving others, you will get stronger, sharper, and happier in every area of your life. "We who are strong ought to bear the infirmities of the weak, and not just to please ourselves."

Day 256 — September 12

IF TODAY IS the best day of your life, remember that it won't last... Or it might be an inch short of hopeless; it won't last either... Whatever has brought you to this moment is only part of the story of your life... Your life is like a tapestry that is uniquely yours... Every choice, every experience is a thread that is woven into a remarkably beautiful work that will be remembered long after you're gone... "There may be tears at night, but joy will come in the morning."

IF YOU HAD one attribute that will bring blessings in your life, ask God to give you faithfulness, because your faithfulness will open the doors to the kingdom of heaven. When I consider all the attributes that God could give to an individual, I find faithfulness at the top of the list. "Well done, good and faithful servant."

Day 257 — September 13

"BRING ME IN remembrance of My word... Let us argue together that you may be proved right." God actually tells us to argue with Him when we believe we are right! And He also says to remind Him of what He says... I think this is so important, and yet I never hear pastors teach on this... So, I am reminding you... Find a scripture that matches your request, remind God, and argue your case...

"THE WORD OF God is healing to all of the flesh." What an amazing promise! So, in other words, just reading the Bible can heal your flesh! Why in the heck aren't we reading the Bible more? Do we believe the Word? Because if we do, and we've got aches and pains or things wrong in our flesh, we need to be reading it more and reminding God of what He said. "Bring Me in remembrance of My word."

Day 258 — September 14

"NEVER DESPISE SMALL beginnings." Small starts are actually powerful, and I believe that we learn more when we start small... "If you're faithful with the little things, you will become ruler over much." Most of the things that God does will start small... The kingdom of God is like a mustard seed, and small will grow if cared for properly...

JESUS HAS THE keys to all the riches of the kingdom of heaven, and He has given those keys to us—not to the world, but to His followers. These riches include everything good in life—financially, spiritually, emotionally, in relationships, and in every other area of life that matters. Ask God to show you how to use this precious inheritance. "And I will give you the keys of the kingdom of heaven."

Day 259 — September 15

"WHEN YOU FEAR the Lord, evil will never be your taskmaster... Calamity will not come near you... "The righteous will rest in times of trouble." Always remember these promises. I love the one that says, "You will only see the reward of the wicked with your eyes, but it will not come near you." I have a feeling that we are going to need these promises. Memorize them and remind God. Our culture is spiraling down at an alarming speed."

EVERY FAMILY HAS "Hidden Generational Treasures" that need to be unearthed and brought to the surface. God's word says that "the blessings come down even to the tenth generation," so we know there are blessings that will drop on us from our ancestors, and it is up to us to dig up those treasures and let them operate in our generation and in the generations that follow us.

Day 260   September 16

"WOE TO THOSE who call evil good and good evil, who put darkness for light and light for darkness, who put bitter for sweet and sweet for bitter." "Fret not" as you watch this coming to pass almost everywhere we look... The darkness and the evil are about to be exposed, and "It's a terrible thing to fall into the hands of the living God." P.S. The word 'woe' is defined as great sorrow or distress...

"SUCCESS IS GETTING up one more time than you are knocked down." Be assured that life will knock you down many times in any given lifespan, and unfortunately, many people will stay down after the first time or two... No matter how many times you find yourself on the mat... Get back up! "Run your race as if to win." A successful life is simply finishing the race on your feet and doing what you know to do. "I can do all things through Christ, who strengthens me."

Day 261 — September 17

THE PARABLES ARE used to actually confuse nonbelievers... God's children hear and understand the parables because He blessed us with the gift of understanding... Proud and religious people will not understand the parables... "Because the knowledge of the secrets of the kingdom of heaven has been given to you, but not to them." If you are having trouble understanding the Word, "Call to Me, I will answer you and show you great and mighty things which you do not know."

BE GENEROUS WITH your prayers and remember that "As you pray one for the other, you are healed yourself." The prayers that you pray over someone can make the difference for them. Your words can be the very thing that moves them toward healing in every area of their life. And "Whatever good thing you do for others, God will do for you." Pray for others!

Day 262 — September 18

"THE KINGDOM OF God is like leaven." It is there in the lump, and it is slowly rising... It is like a hidden seed that is quietly and invisibly germinating... It is also like a hidden treasure that must be unearthed... If you want this wonderful kingdom of God, you must put this above everything else, as you put all your trust in our Father in heaven... "God is the rewarder of those who diligently seek Him."

THE WAY WE steward our lives is what will draw others not only to us but also to God. We can actually be a stumbling block to the unsaved by the way we steward our own lives. Make it a life journey to never be a stumbling block. "Take heed that your liberty does not become a stumbling block to the weak."

Day 263   September 19

IF WE LET a fire burn out of control, it will eventually burn to our back door... And sadly, we don't usually respond until flames are licking at our own back doors... Apathy is a sin, and God says, "It is better to be hot or cold. If you are lukewarm, I will spew you out of My mouth." There is such a thing as a sin of omission. If you see something wrong and it is within your means to do something... Do it!

"LOVE GOD WITH all your heart and soul" and "love others as yourself." All the laws of God hang on these two commandments. Loving God is vertical, as we keep our eyes on Him and put Him first in absolutely everything. And a true love of God will bring about the second commandment, which is horizontal—loving people. When you put these two commandments together, they fulfill the whole law.

Day 264 — September 20

"WHEREVER IS YOUR treasure, there your heart will be also." and "The issues of life flow from the heart." Be cognizant of where you put your treasures, and be sure it is productive, because wherever you put your treasure, your heart will follow and this will establish the direction of your life.

USE THE NAME of Jesus often. People accept the name of God or the Lord, but the name of Jesus is withheld. Be bold with the name of Jesus because it is powerful. "One day every knee will bow to the name of Jesus."

Day 265   September 21

HUMILITY HAS NOTHING to do with putting yourself down or thinking that you are inadequate, but rather, it is lifting God up and realizing that without Him, you are nothing... When you have come to a place in your walk with God where you realize that He is everything and that without Him, you are nothing—but with Him, you are powerful!!! That is when the pure joy of life lives within you... "I can do all things through Christ who strengthens me."

STEPHEN COVEY COINED an amazing phrase that I love... "Begin with the end in mind." Whatever you do in life, if you consider the outcome before you begin, it can save you much pain. Every single choice that we make has a consequence, and if we consider the consequence before the choice, it will set our life on a course of success. "I lay before you life and death, blessing and cursing... Choose life."

Day 266 — September 22

"THE EFFECTUAL FERVENT prayers of a righteous man avails much." ... Today, around the world, 106 million people have committed to praying for America... Please join in and add your fervent prayers to these wonderful people... I believe with all my heart that God hears our prayers, especially when we join together... Even a simple prayer like, "Please help us, Jesus"... And pray that with true fervency... There is power in agreement...

ALWAYS REMEMBER THAT when you keep ugly thoughts in your head, they will eventually show up on your face. Your thoughts have an impact on the muscles of your face, just as they do on the rest of your body. Good thoughts, pretty face... Ugly thoughts, ugly face... Your choice. "Whatever is true or noble, whatever is right or pure, whatever is lovely or admirable... If anything is excellent or praiseworthy... Think on such things."

Day 267   September 23

AS YOU GROW in the Spirit of God, you will be able to experience more of the kingdom of God as you walk out your days... "Taste and see, for the Lord is sweet; blessed is the man that puts his hope in Him." ... A blessing fall on all those who put their hope in God... I know from experience that there is no greater joy than living with Jesus in your heart and walking out your days with a "peace that goes beyond understanding."

WHEN A PROBLEM happens and you aren't sure how to handle it, just do what you know to do, and don't forget that "There is wisdom in many counselors." Ask somebody! I firmly believe that many times we suffer through problems because our pride won't let us ask someone else for help. "Out of the mouth of two or three witnesses, a truth becomes established."

Day 268 — September 24

YOU CANNOT TAKE the goodness of God and then choose to reject Him... "God's compassion rests on everyone," but when you reject Him, you are choosing to separate yourself from the unique blessings that are only for those who choose Him... There is a violent rejection of God in our land today, and as we look around, we see a withdrawal of God's blessings on America... But God will open dominion to those who honor Him, His principles, and His boundaries... Judgment will fall on those who reject Him...

GRATITUDE IS THE highest spiritual form. When we are grateful, it not only totally pleases God, but it makes us feel happy about life. Be intentional about appreciating the things that you have... Praise God and thank Him. When you are grateful, you open the windows of heaven. Stop what you're doing right now and thank God for your health, family, friendships, a sound mind, a roof over your head, and everything else. "In everything, give thanks."

Day 269   September 25

WHEN WE CHOOSE to break through the boundaries that God sets for us, we will destroy our own life… It brings about spiritual and physical disasters when we turn from the path that God has ordained for mankind… We instinctively know when we choose to do wrong, and if we choose it often enough, our heart will become hardened, and we will not be able to hear God… "If you wander from the right path, either to the right or to the left, you will hear a voice behind you saying, 'Stop, go this way.'" … "Today, if you hear His voice, do not harden your heart."

"DRUG OR ALCOHOL abuse can open the doors to demonic influences. We have all witnessed the ravaging of a life by these addictions. But there is hope in Jesus. There have been amazing transformations from these destructive habits. 'Be transformed by the renewal of your mind.' It has been proven that there is no healing from these afflictions without recognizing a higher power. Stay encouraged as you look to God. 'There may be tears at night, but joy will come in the morning.'"

Day 270 September 26

GOD WILL NOT let you perish without offering you the truth first... He is faithful to send us messengers... When someone shares a word with you, first, it must be scriptural, and if you hear it more than once... listen up! The Word says, "Out of the mouth of two or three witnesses, a truth is established." ... And I am a firm believer that you will get a witness in your own spirit as well. "Today, if you hear His voice, do not harden your hearts as in rebellion."

EVIL THRIVES IN darkness and obscurity... but evil cannot operate in the light. Always put light on evil and expose it. Secrets kept hidden in your mind will grow. Share with a trusted friend and expose all evil thoughts. It cannot operate in the light! "Cast down all wild imaginings that try to exalt themselves above the Word of God."

Day 271 September 27

LEARN THE STORY of everyone because they are special just as you are… It is true that some people are just not as interesting as others, but they too have a story to tell, and we need to be gracious and listen to them… Everyone has something to teach us… "When you have done it unto the least of these, my brethren, you have done it unto Me." The way you choose to treat others will always come back on you. Be kind, as you "consider others more important than yourself."

CHOOSING TO SUFFER through a problem by yourself is usually rooted in some sort of pride. God's Word tells us very clearly, "Two are better than one because they have a good reward for their work." He also says, "Woe to him who is alone because he has no one to pick him up when he falls." Do not choose to do life alone. A sorrow shared is half a sorrow, while a joy shared is twice a joy.

Day 272 — September 28

CHRISTIANITY IS NOT a caterpillar with wings... Even though we are a "new creation in Christ," we are not patched up in certain areas... We are brand spanking new!!! "Old things have passed away." ... "You are a brand-new creature in Christ." ... The progression of the new creation is a continuous daily process that continues all the days of our lives... Enjoy the journey...

"THE SEED OF the righteous will always be blessed." That scripture is an amazing promise for your children! Remind God of this scripture as you pray for your children and grandchildren. And remember that as long as you are truly seeking God and have claimed Jesus as your Lord... this scripture belongs to you. I love it!

Day 273   September 29

GOD PROVIDES A physical and spiritual vineyard in our life, and it is our duty to nurture and care for our own vineyard... Do the best you can with what you have... God provides everything for a strong and fruitful life... Many of us start out with a very small little patch, but if you take care of what you have, it will prosper and grow... And watch the little things in life because they are the things that, when compiled, make the big things... "It is the little foxes that ruin the vines."

"IN PEACE I will both lie down and sleep, for You alone, O Lord, make me dwell in safety." God promises His people "sweet sleep," and He tells us to remind Him of what He says. If you are one of the millions of Christians who do not sleep well at night... try reminding God of this special promise before you go to sleep... And every time you wake up in the night, remind Him again... And then "believe you have received." Sweet sleep, my friends.

Day 274 — September 30

GOD'S WORD IS a sword, and it should be used often... God's declarations and promises are "sharper than a two-edged sword, piercing even to the division of soul, spirit, and joints." It is our only offensive weapon, and it is all we need... But you must learn these promises and declarations, and then speak them out of your mouth with the authority given to you in the name of Jesus.

I WAS RECENTLY asked, what was my favorite scripture? After much consideration and knowing the deep love I have for the Bible in general, I decided upon one scripture—Romans 8:28: "And we know that in all things God works for the good of those who love Him and who have been called according to His purpose." When we spend our life seeking to serve God, this promise is all-encompassing. There is nothing more comforting than knowing that no matter what happens... it will work toward good. What a great promise.

I OFTEN TO call my mom and tell her how much I will miss her when she is gone. I'll blubber like an idiot, telling her how much I love her, how much fun our journey has been. When that day comes, I will have said everything a son can say to his mother. And while I will grieve, I will do so with a smile on my face knowing she will be in heaven. Mom's books are a lasting legacy for all of us as she shares from life experiences. She is truly an overcomer. Her books are Holy Spirit-inspired. Simply put, my mom and I do life together—we know everything going on in each other's life. As you read this book, her thoughts, insight, love, and wisdom will leap off the pages at just the right time. Mom loves people and I know she is praying that your life will be transformed by the power and blood of Jesus Christ. This book is indeed a *Secret Treasure in Plain Sight*. Godspeed.

– Eric Solis, Son

 # October

Day 275   October 1

WE ARE ALL given a special character at the time of our birth, and it takes a lifetime to completely develop that character... Whether you are overly boisterous or painfully shy, you have to manage what God has given you... It is never wise to let your extreme personality run rampant... Take charge of who you are as you maximize and fine-tune your character gifts and flaws... "God is faithful to finish the work He has started in you." ... Do your part...

CLOSE THE DISTANCE between you and Jesus. "Draw close to Him, and He will draw close to you."

Day 276 — October 2

THINK OF THE "space in between" as a present suffering that will bring about the expectation of a new life. Life itself is filled with tension. Violence is the norm on this earth, and we can see this by observing nature itself. We spend our lives trying to tame the natural course of tension and violence as we deal with the troubles in this life... But with God, we have hope, and we know that we are "saved by grace," and at the end of this life, we will ascend into Heaven, where "the lambs will lie down with the lions," and we will receive our promised redemption. Yippee!

A NEW LIFE requires a new lifestyle... You cannot put the new in with the old because your newness will get diluted and eventually burst, akin to "putting new wine in old wineskins." ... The new will be lost if it's kept in the old... You are not who you used to be if you are born again... You have a new nature within you... "The one who practices sin is not a child of God." ... Although we all sin daily, we cannot continuously choose to walk in a sinful lifestyle, or we will be judged accordingly...

Day 277　　　　　　　　　　　　October 3

PRESENT SUFFERING BRINGS future glory. As we go through trials, we should be filled with expectation. Just as labor pains bring the joy of the birth of a child… there are many times that pain is the only way to find the glorious outcome. Pain and suffering often bring new life. Stand strong and trust God as you walk out your life journey. "There may be tears at night, but joy will come in the morning." This too shall pass.

THE BIBLE SAYS God first destroyed the earth by water and promised never to do so again (the true meaning of the rainbow). He said, "I will destroy it by fire the second time." I don't fully understand Revelation, but I do know I want to spend eternity in Heaven. The rapture comes before the Antichrist.

I've heard of Christ's second coming since childhood—AI, microchips, digital currency, and government control all align with the "Mark of the Beast." While we're busy with life, these things go unnoticed. We see it unfolding daily. While the devil prepares people for the Antichrist, God prepares people for the rapture. I don't know when it will happen, but I don't plan to be left behind. God is giving us a chance to repent. Until He calls me home, I declare Jesus Christ as the one true Savior. Though I fail, I believe in Him. If you're not ashamed, copy this as your status. I believe in God the Father, Jesus the Son, and the Holy Spirit. Amen.

Day 278 — October 4

WHAT IF YOU could??? What if you had the opportunity to do something that you thought you could never do... Would you give it a shot? Or would you cower away, thinking that you're not capable? God's Word tells us, "I can do all things through Christ, who strengthens me." ... Do you believe that God could give you the ability to do something that He has dropped into your spirit? Nothing ventured, nothing gained... "God works in you to will and to do His good pleasure." I say, GO FOR IT!!!

EVERY DISADVANTAGE HAS an advantage." In God's kingdom, there has to be a disadvantage before there is a miracle, and I love miracles! When you recognize that there is some sort of disadvantage in your life, work with it in a creative way and find the advantage. There is an advantage there if you look for the "hidden treasure in a dark secret place."

Day 279   October 5

TEACHERS OPEN THE door, but you must enter by yourself." Teachers have to be learners. When you choose to be a teacher, God will hold you more responsible, but you will also be given more of everything. It is such a blessing to give, and teaching is giving. Be sure that you are called to be a teacher before you take on this noble position. "To him that much is given, much is expected."

THIS IS TRUE and wise, but true wisdom should also bring you closer to God. As Judi Dench says: *"Don't prioritize your looks, my friend—they won't last. But your humor, intuition, and ability to choose your battles will only grow. Your capacity for stillness and living in the moment will blossom. Your instinct for knowing what and who is worth your time will flourish. Prioritize what makes you unique—the invisible magnet that draws in like-minded souls. These are the things that will only get better."*

Day 280 — October 6

ONE WAY OR another, all of us will have to reckon with who Jesus is and what He means to us. *"One day every knee will bow."* It is clear that the end times are drawing near. God help those who have not taken the time to know Jesus. My prayer is that all would come to the knowledge of their Savior. *"Many are called, but few are chosen."* Those who reject Him are not chosen—it is your choice.

IT IS NOT so much what you see, but how you see it that matters. *"Beauty is in the eye of the beholder."* I love the old adage that even in the mud and scum of things, something will sing. Choose to see the beauty in everything—it is often a hidden treasure that must be sought. Finding that beauty will bring joy to your heart.

Day 281   October 7

BOOKER T WASHINGTON once said, "A lie does not become truth... Wrong does not become right... Evil does not become good just because the majority believes it." In our culture today, lies run rampant, good has become evil, and wrong is everywhere we look... Do not allow yourself to believe anything that tries to exalt itself above God's Word... Stand on what you know to be true and keep looking up as you stand on the promises of protection for your family... "One day, every knee will bow."

ANGER IS AN outward manifestation of either fear, hurt, or frustration, and life itself has good reason to bring about all of the above... But remember that "anger will never accomplish the purposes of God." In fact, I love the old adage that says, "You get more flies with honey than vinegar." "A gentle answer turns away wrath." Anger is nothing more than kindling thrown into a raging fire that can set your life on a course of destruction!!!

Day 282 — October 8

A MAN IS not defeated when he has lost... He's only defeated when he quits... I love that motto... Defeat is never bad! At the very worst, it is a wonderful lesson... People are so quick to throw in the towel and give up... God's Word says, "Something quickly gotten is quickly lost, but amassed little by little, it has great value." "Grow not weary of well-doing because, in due season, you shall have your reward."

WE ARE LIVING in the tension of a fallen world. Just as we see the violence displayed by wild animals in their natural habitat, such is the natural environment of our world. "We are of this world, but it is not our home." When we receive Jesus as our Lord, He will help us journey through this time of frailty in a troubled, fallen world. Stand strong and trust God as you walk out your life journey.

Day 283   October 9

WE ARE ALL born with the same measure of faith, and what we do with that faith depends on its power... "Faith comes by hearing the word of God." So your choice is to build your faith up by reading the Word and causing it to be a powerhouse by using it. Everyone has the same opportunity to build their faith, and faith is what brings about the miracles of life...

HOPE CAN CAUSE someone to break through, and I believe that hope can even heal a person. Be determined to give people hope when they are in your sphere of influence. The hope you give can cause a person's faith to rise up, and that faith can lead to wholeness in the flesh and the spirit. Hope will bring a person into the light. "A word aptly spoken is like apples of gold in settings of silver."

Day 284 — October 10

IF YOU ARE not content with what you have now, you will not be content with what you now want... The opposite of contentment is covetousness, which is a sin... Cleave to and cultivate contentment... Choose to love what is yours, and if you take care of it and enjoy it, God will give you more... "Godliness with contentment is great gain."

WHEN YOU CHOOSE to lay up all your riches in worldly goods... When this life ends, you will be stripped naked... Nothing from this life goes with you... All souls belong to God, and all of us will make an account to God... Your life does not merely consist of your riches in this life... "What does it profit a man to gain the whole world and lose his soul?" If your soul is not prospering, you are a fool in God's eyes.

Day 285   October 11

THERE ARE THINGS in your life that you must forgive and forget in order to successfully move forward... Hanging on to old hurts and unforgiveness is detrimental to your progress... "Forget the things that are behind and move towards the things that are ahead." Move forward with a positive thought as you expect good things to happen... "As you believe, so you are."

HARDSHIPS WILL HUMBLE the proud heart, and we will all have breakdowns in our lives... When you find a breakdown in your life, fall at the feet of Jesus. Jesus is the hope that breaks through all boundaries. Hope in Jesus will break through all isolation, tragedy, and chaos. "Those who put their trust in God will never be disappointed."

Day 286   October 12

THERE ARE SOME things you can change and other things you have no control over... Don't waste your time lamenting over things that you cannot change... Ask God to help you organize the tasks in your life that need attention, and then allow Him to "make your path straight." Remember that perfect order brings perfect peace... Get things in order because we serve an orderly God...

SOMETIMES THERE ARE circumstances in life that are so troubling that we push them down deep and move on with a façade in front of us. As the years go by, the circumstance may surface in different ways and oftentimes in dreams. This is a perfect time to use the phrase, "Let go and let God." Embrace the issue and don't run from it. God is working a healing on your behalf as He exposes your deepest hurts. "There may be tears at night, but joy will come in the morning." Hallelujah.

Day 287 October 13

CULTIVATE CONTENTMENT RATHER than covetousness... If you are not living in contentment, you are poor and destitute no matter how much earthly riches you may have... "The love of money is the root of all evil." It is not the money that is evil, but rather the love of money... Almost every sin known to mankind is somehow rooted in the love of money!!! Choose contentment... That is the real riches of life...

THERE ARE MANY people who seem to do well for long seasons of their lives while completely ignoring God. They are comfortable in their own little world... But the day will come when they will need Jesus. "Be careful when you think you stand, lest you fall." "The grass will wither, and the flower will fade," and something is bound to break. "One day, every knee will bow."

Day 288   October 14

LEARN TO RECOGNIZE the voice of God... You can learn to listen spiritually... He talks to us in many ways... Sometimes through people, the Bible, confirmation through two or three different people, or just a gentle urging in our own spirit... Many times, I know it's Him because it will be something that I would not have thought of or done... And remember: "The wisdom of God is first pure and then peaceful." When you don't have peace about something... Don't proceed!!

"FORGETTING THE THINGS that are behind and looking towards the things that are ahead." There are several seasons throughout our lifetime when everything seems to change. We adjust to gradual changes throughout our lives, but every once in a while, it seems that everything changes at once. It doesn't do any good to cling to the familiar... Flow with the change, as "God directs your steps."

Day 289　　　　　　　　October 15

THERE ARE MANY counterfeits in our lives, and they usually appear to be very much like the real thing... They often come just before the real thing... Be careful of counterfeits... "If you have a doubt, back out." I believe that God will alert us when we have learned to hear His voice... "Call to me, and I will answer you, and will tell you great and hidden things that you have not known."

THERE IS NO addiction, failure, or regret that God cannot overturn. It is only God and the blood of Jesus that can "turn your mourning into dancing." I firmly believe that there are many addictions and failures that cannot be healed without Jesus... Don't give up, but you have to push into Him to be able to stay clean. You got this!

Day 290 — October 16

JUST BECAUSE YOU are going through a storm does not mean that you are under judgment... "In this world, you will have trouble, but take heart, for I have overcome this world."... Trouble will come and go throughout your life, but if you put your trust in God, it will soon pass... I love the scripture that says, "There may be tears at night, but joy will come in the morning."... When you lay down at night after a rough day, remind God of this beautiful scripture... Then expect joy in the morning...

CLOSE THE DISTANCE between you and Jesus. "Draw close to Him, and He will draw close to you." Stay close to God through prayer, gratitude, and acknowledgment. A simple prayer of "Help me, Jesus" will work wonders... "Call unto Me, and I will answer."

Day 291   October 17

UNTIL WE STOP making excuses for ourselves, we will never be healed of our issues... Be willing to embrace your shortcomings or admit when you've done something wrong... It is so immature to say, "I did it because..." If it's wrong, it doesn't matter why you did it, and there's nothing more frustrating than this childish response... The simple answer is to say, "I was wrong, and I'm sorry." This will save so much bickering... "If it can be done, as much as possible on your part, live in peace with all men."

ONCE WE ARE deeply rooted in God, nothing will shake us loose from the trust that we have built through our relationship with Him. "We will be like a tree planted by the water that nothing will shake." There is such peace and comfort in knowing that you know that you know that God is real... "Draw close to Him, and He will draw close to you."

Day 292 — October 18

WE WILL HAVE to learn to live and deal with evil during this season until the fullness of God's kingdom is completely revealed... When Jesus comes back, the aspect of judgment will be the separation of the evil from the good... I pray that all of us will be on His right side with the sheep rather than with the goats on His left... "Be not deceived, God is not mocked; as a man sows, so shall he reap."

HARD WORK HAS become a lost virtue in our culture. It seems that people don't want to work today... Or they want to get by with just doing as little as they have to... God's word clearly tells us that He "blesses the work of our hands." Hard work produces its own reward: "The hard-working farmer gets the first pick of the crops." If you're not keeping your hands moving and working hard, don't complain about not being blessed.

Day 293   October 19

GOD TELLS US 365 times in the Bible to: "Be strong and courageous." Remember that courage isn't always loud; sometimes, it's quiet courage that just goes forward in the wake of danger... It just quietly does what needs to be done, even if the flesh is frightened... A hero is just an ordinary person who responds when needed... One who isn't concerned about themselves, one who will put themselves at risk to rescue someone else... "Be strong and courageous."

"BE ALL THINGS to all people that you may win some to the Lord." Meet people right where they are. Discern where they are in their walk before you try to beat them over the head with the Bible. Sometimes people are ready to receive right from the beginning, while others may take weeks, months, or even years. Stay the course and be patient as you "consider others more important than yourself."

Day 294   October 20

WORDS CAN CHANGE a life, whether it be for good or bad... "The tongue has the power of life and death." Make a commitment to speak of the goodness of God... "Let no corrupt communication come out of your mouth." Sometimes a simple word of encouragement can actually change a life that seems doomed... Be that one who speaks those positive words... We all need encouragement...

THE PEN IS mightier than the sword... The written word is accepted and believed even if it does not have any verified backing... People often quote something they read somewhere... The written word is usually nothing more than "one man's opinion," unless it has facts to back it up... Lies are rampant... I love what Ronald Reagan used to say: "Trust, but verify."

Day 295 October 21

"HATE IN OUR thoughts generates a deadly poison in the body that kills if it is not neutralized by love. Where there is hate, there can be no health, no success, no happiness... Hate works evil to him who holds it, and hate is the thickest veil of all!" We wonder why people cannot see things that seem so clear? Hate blocks blessings from our eyes!

BE NOT DECEIVED, bad company corrupts good behavior. When you mingle with people who are negative, disrespectful, arrogant, prideful, angry, and contrary to God and his principles, you are taking a chance of being tainted by them. While it is good to be kind to unbelievers and even try to set a good example for them, it is not good to yoke yourself with them or spend too much time in their presence. "As iron sharpens iron, so a man sharpens the countenance of his friend." Be careful who you allow to influence your countenance.

Day 296 — October 22

GOD CAN AND does do miracles in the trials of life... In fact, the messes in life are generally where a miracle is needed... Ask God to bring about a miracle in an area that seems hopeless, and then recognize and acknowledge God when he does create a miracle... "Weren't there ten healed and yet only one came back to say thank you?" Be that one who always thanks God for what he has done in your life.

WE CAN ONLY receive more faith by the word of God. "Faith comes by hearing the word of God." The faith you receive comes from reading and hearing the word. However, you can build faith muscle by using, sharing, and praying in the spirit. "We are all given the same measure of faith." But it is up to you to build up your own faith.

Day 297   October 23

"HE WILL YET fill your mouth with laughter and your lips with shouts of joy." This is one of those hidden treasures that needs to be memorized and called out... Remember that God tells us to "Bring me in remembrance of my word." When you're feeling low or depressed, remind God of that beautiful promise... "You have not because you ask not."

THE ENEMY WILL put walls in front of us... Walls of isolation, humiliation, loneliness, or financial burdens... He uses all sorts of things to try to wall us in... But King David, on his deathbed, said out loud, "Oh my God, for it is by you I have run through a troop, and by you, I have leapt over a wall." He stopped on his deathbed and remembered all that God had brought him through... There is no wall that the enemy can put in front of you that God will not bring you over, through, or around. "What the enemy means for evil, God will turn to good."

Day 298 — October 24

DISCONNECTING FROM OTHERS is a sign of moving away from God... Strong connections with others is healthy, both spiritually and physically... Do not do life alone!!! "It is not good for man to be alone because if he falls, he has no one to pick him up." We are called by God to live a connected life... "Two are better than one because they have a good reward for their work." Share your life with others.

OFTEN TIMES, SUFFERING brings about great joy, just as labor pains bring about the joy of the birth of a child. "Count it all joy when you go through fiery trials because it is perfecting you." There are many times that pain is the only way to find the glorious outcome. Pain and agony often bring new life. "There may be tears at night, but joy will come in the morning."

Day 299 — October 25

"THE HUMAN MIND plans the way, but the Lord directs the steps." When you put your trust in the Lord, He promises that "He will direct your steps." It is still our part to plan our days, but when your plans are interrupted, be at peace and trust that God has changed your direction... What a great feeling to know that everything that happens to you is planned by the One who knows what is best for you...

EVERY VERSE IN the Bible is either a promise, a principle, a parable, a prophecy, or a prohibition. There are over 6,000 promises and 600 prohibitions or laws... There are 324 direct and fulfilled prophecies about Jesus and many more prophetic words about the world we live in. Jesus gave us many analogies in His parables, and of course, the books of Proverbs and Ecclesiastes are filled with Godly principles. "Study to show yourself approved."

Day 300 — October 26

"HE WHO KEEPS instruction is in the way of life, but he who refuses correction goes astray." I think many of us are guilty of this... It would behoove all of us to pay attention to wise correction... The Word also tells us that "the wise man learns by watching, but the fool has to have a rod taken to his back." Be willing to receive correction or even learn how to do something a better way than "your way"... (I hear You, Lord. 😣)

THE ABILITY TO deal with adversity and have resilience is probably one of the most coveted attributes. If we would put the same effort towards finding a solution instead of whining and complaining, life would be so much easier. "Fret not, it will only cause harm." I love these three words... Figure it out!

Day 301   October 27

PRAY FOR CONFUSION for the enemy... Just as Jehovah was told by God to go fight the Moabites, and when he got there, they were all dead because they were confused and fought each other... Remember that talking in circles and word salads are a form of confusion... Be sure and thank God when you see an answer to your prayer... "Ask and you shall receive."

WHEN YOU GIVE, give your best. When you give out of your need, it is imputed to you as great faith. When you give out of your abundance, it is still good, but giving out of your need always produces more. Wherever your needs lie, give in that area, and God will bless your socks off. "With whatever measure you use to give, it will be measured back to you."

Day 302   October 28

EINSTEIN ONCE SAID, "Negative people find a problem for every solution." We all know that person that we try to help with a positive suggestion, and they tell you why it won't work... There are characters that just seem to think negatively, but it is imperative that you learn your character and manage it... If you happen to be one of those people, work hard to see the positive in everything. "I can do all things through Christ who strengthens me."

WHEN YOU ARE troubled, don't pray for deliverance from your problem but rather ask God that you will fulfill your purpose in your problem. "Count it all joy when you go through the fiery trials because it is perfecting you." Yes, ask God to "give you the strength sufficient for today." But embrace the problem and work your way through it as you learn the lessons that will ultimately strengthen you. If you run from your problem, it will follow you. Stay put and work through them.

Day 303   October 29

THERE ARE TIMES that you can be right in the middle of God's will, and yet everything in hell is coming against you... A closed door can be God's will! It does not mean that things are not progressing as they should... "There is a time and a season for everything under the sun." Just as fruit on a tree has a process of ripening, so it goes with the events in your life... Stand strong, don't quit, and trust God... "There may be tears at night, but joy will come in the morning."

IT IS SAID that the world is going to hell in a handbasket... Well, my answer to that is... It probably is, but the Christians are "going to heaven in the twinkling of an eye." I am not sure if we are at that point... But I will tell you this much, the point that Jesus returns will look exactly like it looks today... Every single thing is lined up, nothing missing! Be sure that you have made Jesus the Lord of your life... I would not want to be on this planet after the Christians are gone! Come, sweet Jesus.

Day 304   October 30

SOMETIMES THE GREATEST blessings of all go unnoticed as we take our good life for granted... We in America walk in tremendous blessings every day of our life... We see people burning flags and rioting because they are ungrateful! "Start each day with a grateful heart." Gratefulness brings blessings into your life... While the ungrateful heart is never satisfied...

THE CIRCUMSTANCES OF your life should never make the difference between whether you are grateful or not. There are all kinds of things that can happen throughout a lifetime, and many of them are not good... But God has His hand on you, and if you continue to praise Him and thank Him, even in the face of a trial, He will work those things towards good. "All things work together for good to those who love God and are called according to His purpose."

Day 305   October 31

THE DIFFERENCE BETWEEN winners and losers is that winners are willing to do what losers don't want to do... I always say that, generally speaking, the "have-nots" are the "do-nots." **"THE DILIGENT HAND** shall become ruler over much." Those who are not willing to do the work are usually the ones who end up with a mediocre life and never really go anywhere... It takes nerve, hard work, creative ideas, and a positive attitude to get your head above the crowd...

OUR RELATIONSHIP WITH God is the most essential need we have. Secondly is our relationship with family. When our lives are out of line with God or our family, it can throw our whole life out of whack. "With whatever is within you, be at peace with all men." And always be at peace with your God... You will never know true joy until you know your Father in heaven and how much He loves you.

ONE LAST THING I would like to add to all the wonderful things said about Mom is what makes her so unique and special. This may be hard to fathom, but Mom has not always been the confident and courageous woman you know today—nor that pillar of strength whom you wait for daily, anticipating the ding on your phone just to receive another dose of wisdom that keeps you centered on the eternal rather than the temporal.

On the contrary, Mom had a very traumatic upbringing that left her riddled with every kind of fear imaginable. Throughout my childhood, she struggled with severe anxiety and frequent panic attacks. Safety and security were far from my reality growing up—until she cried out to Jesus and surrendered her broken and shattered life to Him. I witnessed firsthand how God can take a wounded soul and transform it into a strong, healthy tower of strength—one that many now depend on to receive Spirit-filled words of empowerment and encouragement. Only God can take our weakness and turn it into our strength!

When Mom shares the living Word of God with us, she speaks with strong conviction because she knows firsthand what God's promises are and what they can do if you just believe and act on that faith. Mighty mountains can be moved, and giants that grip us with fear and addiction can be conquered—all in the mighty name of Jesus! Enjoy these delightful tidbits of nourishment that will inspire and encourage your daily walk as you fight the "good fight of faith!"

– **Stacey Solis Mills**

November

Day 306   November 1

THE ROAD TO the promised land goes right through the wilderness... We don't make it to our personal promised land without the trials of life... Trials and the wilderness are part of our life journey, and without them, the learning process is not complete... But I also love the promise that says, "Everyone born of God can expect victory." If you stand strong and don't waver, "You will see the goodness of God in the land of the living."

MAKE WHAT YOU believe is the best decision and move forward. Even if it is incorrect, God will guide you as you go. Just keep moving and remember that God promises that when you "acknowledge Him, He will direct your steps," and then trust that He has. Even a bumpy road can get you where you're supposed to be.

Day 307 — November 2

YOUR PRAISE AND gratefulness should never be circumstantial. "This is the day the Lord has made, and I will rejoice and be glad in it." Jesus told us, "In this world, you will have problems, but I have overcome the problems." I firmly believe that no matter what is going on in your life, if you wake up and praise the Lord out loud, your days will be good, and your boundaries will be gentle.

LIFE IS NOT just about you!!! When something happens that affects you, it is wise to note the value that it may have for others…God has a whole myriad of considerations and some of the consequences may not appear to be beneficial for you, but if you truly Love God and you are walking in his purpose for you… No matter what happens "It will work towards good!"

Day 308 — November 3

NEVER DOUBT IN the dark what God has shown you in the light... Remind yourself of past victories for yourself and others... "God is no respecter of persons; what He does for one, He will do for another." When you read about a victory in the Bible, remember that if He did it for them, He can do it for you... Remind God of that when you hear or read something... He tells us to, "Bring Me in remembrance of My Word." "You have not because you ask not."

"FACTS ARE STUBBORN things, and your opinion cannot change the facts." There are those who, no matter what kind of proof you give them, are more impressed with their own opinion than with the truth... This is a sad place to find yourself... Always be willing to listen to others, then consider and verify what they say. "There is wisdom in many counselors."

Day 309   November 4

WHEN YOU THINK others are more blessed than you... It is only because they have sought more of God's blessings than you... "Draw close to God, and He will draw close to you."... We are all given the same measure of blessing at our birth, and just as a well-tended garden produces beautiful fruit, so it goes with your unique blessings... "He who tends the tree enjoys the fruit thereof."

WE OFTEN TALK about a wall falling that is in front of us... But the scripture says that there are times when God will cause you to leap over a wall! Many times, the wall is not going to go anywhere... There are some things that men cannot do, "but with God, all things are possible." There is no wall that God cannot bring you through, over, or around... Trust Him.

Day 310   November 5

GOD WILL TAKE down our enemies... "The Lord will fight for you; you need only be still."... "It is not by might, and not by strength, but by My Spirit, says the Lord."... There may be a silent period where you think that God is not going to take them down, but in due season, they will stumble and fall... Keep the arm of your flesh out of the way and put your trust in God...

THE WORD GRACE means that God is giving us something that we don't deserve. But I have coined a phrase that I call "enabling grace." It is used for those things in our lives that, on our own, we would not be able to do, but because of God's enabling grace, "we can do all things through Christ, who strengthens us." The next time something arises that you are singularly unable to do, ask God for His enabling grace. I walk through this life with that blessing covering me every day.

Day 311   November 6,

"GOD IS DOING all sorts of things that you are unable to see... He is always working for your good. "You will see the greatness of the Lord in the land of the living." Sometimes your biggest blessing is having God defeat your enemies... He tells us, "No weapon formed against you will prosper." When people come against you and you are a child of God, you will be protected, you will have the answer to their interrogation, and they will fall into the pit that they dug for you..."

SERVE OTHERS EVEN if you feel empty. "God's power is made strong in your weakness." Your strength and provision will soar when you serve others. "God will give you the strength sufficient for the day." When you pour yourself out, you will find that service leads to refreshing, refilling, and redirecting. When you give and serve with everything you have, you will feel so refreshed. "Those who are to become great in the kingdom of God must first become servants to all."

Day 312 November 7

GOD BLESSES EVERYONE, and it is up to us to maintain and enjoy that blessing... When you do not respect or are not grateful for that blessing, the blessing will lift off of you... Those who grab hold of that universal blessing given to all men will benefit, and the blessing will increase... "Draw close to God, and He will draw close to you."

WORDS CAN CHANGE the world. Harsh words can destroy, while gentle, encouraging words are "like apples of gold in settings of silver." Speak life! We live in a toxic environment—be the one to help change the world with kind words. Whatever good words you have to give and share... give them and share them. When you choose to bless others, God will bless you, and what God blesses, nothing can harm.

Day 313   November 8

IF YOU EVER doubt God, stop and remember what He has done in your life... We often forget that every little thing that is good in our life came from God... "All good things come from above." We tend to take God for granted as we have expectations for the things we need and want... We have so many blessings that we don't even recognize... "In everything give thanks."

OFTEN TIMES BLESSINGS and problems walk hand in hand. I've always found in my own life that blessings usually came from my biggest problems. Problems can be similar to the pruning of a tree—it is necessary for the tree to produce beautiful new life. So, it is with our lives... Pruning can be painful, but it is also very productive... "Be strong and courageous" as you work through your daily issues, doing what you know to do and trusting that God is "directing your steps."

Day 314 — November 9

"THE SOUL OF a lazy man desires and has nothing, but the soul of the diligent shall be made rich."... We live in a culture where people feel entitled to share in the wealth of others... The Word makes it very clear: "If a man doesn't work, a man doesn't eat." There are definite times that we need to help people, but more often than not, it is the slothful who are needy... Be diligent with what is yours, and you will always have enough...

NO MATTER WHAT the world brings into your life, maintain a fresh, reverent faith in God. Jesus said, "In this world, you will have trouble, but I have overcome the world." Trust the Lord with all your heart. There is nowhere else to go. As we travel our journey, we often can't understand what and why God is allowing something. But as you move along your path and look back on your life... Most times, you will be able to see more clearly what God was doing. "His ways are higher than our ways, and His thoughts are higher than our thoughts."

Day 315   November 10

"CALL TO ME and I will show you great and mighty things... Things you do not know of."... Wow! I love this one... When was the last time that you called out to God and asked Him to show you great and mighty things? Remember, He tells us to remind Him of what He says... How about we try this today? Heavenly Father, we are collectively calling out to You as we read this message... Show us great and mighty things in the name of Jesus. Amen...

CHOOSE THE JOYS of life, and they will choose you. Choose to see and remember the good things. Life is filled with all sorts of magical wonder, and yet it is also interspersed with all sorts of ugly messes. I love the scripture Philippians 4:8 that says, "Whatever things are just, pure, lovely, of a good report, if there be any virtue, and if there be any praise, think on these things." Choose to see the beauty.

Day 316 — November 11

WE CANNOT HONESTLY call ourselves Christians if we are not willing to abide by the principles of God's Word... We have to be willing to lay aside the ways of the world and deny ourselves... This does not mean that we cannot have fun, but it does mean that we stay within the perimeters of God's Word... "Blessed are those who acclaim You and walk in the light of Your presence, Lord."

WHEN YOUR ANSWER is delayed, do not give up—just "stand and believe." Even if your hope dies, keep believing. What a difference a day can make when hope is stirred up, and many times, it is up to us to stir up our own hope. I always ask God to encourage me or encourage others because encouragement brings hope, and we have to have hope to have strong faith... And as we know, faith is what activates God's Word in our lives. Stand strong and "only believe."

Day 317   November 12

"BLESSED IS THE one who trusts in the Lord, whose confidence is in Him... They will be like a tree planted by the water that sends out its roots by the stream... It does not fear when heat comes; its leaves are always green... It has no worries in a year of drought and never fails to bear fruit... I adore this beautiful promise, and I often remind God of it when I'm praying for others as well as for myself... Remember to remind God of His promises."

WITHIN THE COVERS of the Bible are the answers to all the problems that men face, and yet millions of dollars are spent on all sorts of things seeking those answers. There are those who go to therapists for years and never once open the Bible. God thought of everything when the Bible was composed, and a good therapist would include His plan... or better yet, take your issues right to God... "Call unto Me, and I will deliver you from all of your problems."

Day 318   November 13

WE ARE LIVING in a time where good and evil are coexisting... But be not deceived, God is still working, and one day evil will be eradicated. There will be a time of harvest, and God will separate us from the evil. Stay encouraged as you pray God's protective promises for you and your family. "You will only see the reward of the wicked with your eyes, but it will not come near you." I love that promise!

JUST BECAUSE YOU'RE going through storms and troubles does not mean you are in the wrong place. Many times, God uses your storms to show you your own potential and His power. "God's power is made strong in your weakness." Storms can slow you down, and many times the storm will hold you back from your calling and your destiny. God uses these storms to develop character and potential. "Grow not weary of well-doing, because in due season you shall have your reward."

Day 319 — November 14

"OH TASTE AND see that the Lord is good." Raise your hands and give everything over to God. There are many in our country who are celebrating, while others are hurting over the election. The sad part is that both sides feel equally as positive that they are the ones who are right. There are splits in families and friendships over this subject, and it should NEVER be. Never give up a loved one for a politician! We all have the right to our opinion. Let's respect each other's opinions as we move forward with majority rule. We are so blessed to live in a country where we can still choose. Thank God!

WHEN LIFE IS easy and things are in abundance, the nature is to move farther away from God. But during times of trouble, we tend to look to God and fall at His feet. So consequently, God allows some things in our life to bring us closer to Him. It is easier and wiser to look to God daily, whether you abase or abound. Life is just simpler and more fun when you put your trust in God. I know this because I have tried both ways.

Day 320   November 15

"SEEK FIRST THE kingdom of God and His righteousness, and all other things will be added." There are over 6,000 promises in the Bible, and this is one of them. When we choose to obey God and stay within the perimeters of what He requires of us, we almost don't need to ask for anything else because everything will be added. Choose to follow the path that God has laid before you and live your life at peace as God provides all of your needs.

IMAGINED OPPOSITION CAN often be our biggest foe.

"Most of my fears I have cured,
The sharpest ones I have survived,
But the hardest of all to endure
Are those evils that never arrived."

ALL OF US have spent wasted time worrying about something that never happened… "Therefore, do not worry about tomorrow, for tomorrow will worry about itself. Sufficient to the day is its own trouble." Savor today.

Day 321   November 16

WE CANNOT EXPECT Jesus to fit into our arranged life. We are called to fit into His arranged order. We cannot be His disciple unless we are willing to adapt to His ways. Yes, you can get your ticket to heaven by simply confessing Jesus as your Lord, but in order to share in His amazing promises in the land of the living, there is much more required. "If you are faithful to the end, I will award you with a glorious life." I don't know about you, but I want that glorious life... And so far, so good! ⊠

"IN THE MUD and scum of things, something, something always sings." I love this line, and it is taken from a poem by Ralph Waldo Emerson. But it is also a biblical statement. God's creation is magical if you take the time to really enjoy it. "God has made everything beautiful in His time." God created a beautiful world, and men have done lots of damage to it... But the beauty is still everywhere you look. "Beauty is in the eye of the beholder."

Day 322 — November 17

YOUR SECURITY LIES in doing God's will. "Obedience is better than sacrifice." When you have chosen to do things God's way, no matter what comes at you, you will be rescued by God. Honor God, and you can rest assured that He will always take care of you. What an amazing promise!

WILLIAM PENN ONCE said, "A true friend unbosoms freely, advises justly, assists readily, adventures boldly, takes all patiently, defends courageously, and continues a friend unchangeably." There is nothing like a true friend who sticks closer than a brother. God's Word tells us, "It's not good for man to be alone, because if he falls, he has no one to pick him up." Treasure your friends! And remember, "For a person to have friends, they must show themselves friendly."

Day 323   November 18

APPOINT YOUR DAYS ahead of time... There comes a time in life when you need to shake up your life, shut down the old, and renew everything. Renovate everything as you honor God in your restoration. "Behold, I'm about to do something new... See, I have already begun... I will make a pathway in the wilderness and streams in the desert." Wait for it and watch for it as you do your part to make it happen.

BENJAMIN FRANKLIN ONCE said, "By failing to prepare, you are preparing to fail." God's Word tells us to be prepared, not out of fear, but out of wisdom. He mentions the ants and tells us, "They have no commander, no leader, no ruler, yet they store their provisions in summer and gather their food at harvest." We are living in a time when it is just wise to be prepared. It is wonderful to be a Pollyanna and see things through rose-colored glasses, but it's also wise to be aware of what's happening around us. Watch the ants!

Day 324   November 19

"SEEK FIRST THE kingdom of God and His righteousness, and everything else shall be added." God deserves our first and our best. Start your day with a praise, a prayer, or a song. When you begin your day with an acknowledgment of God, everything else in your life will fall into place. "Honor God with your first fruits, and your barns will be filled with plenty, and your vats will be bursting with new wine."

IT IS SAID that overnight success takes about 15 years. There are many who never reach their pinnacle of success because they are not willing to wait. Remember that quitters never win, and winners never quit. "Those who wait upon the Lord shall renew their strength; they shall rise up with wings like eagles, they shall run and not grow weary, they shall walk and not faint."

Day 325   November 20

GOD WILL ALWAYS allow free choice! People ask, "Why does God let that happen?" Because God has given mankind the right to choose, and He will never thwart your right to choose... And unfortunately, these choices have caused much pain and disasters to mankind. He says, "I lay before you life and death, blessing and cursing... Choose life." And even though He tells us to choose life and blessing, oft times men choose death and cursing. Be sure, as you consider your choices, to "choose life."

SOMEWHERE IN OUR struggles, there is a revelation of Jesus. It is often in the midst of our struggles that God will lift a veil and "show us great and mighty things, things we did not know." God uses intense struggles to reveal Himself in the way we need to see Him, usually in a time of aloneness, and others may not even get it. One of these glimpses of Jesus will change us forever. We can only receive these revelations during intense struggles. "There may be tears at night, but joy will come in the morning."

Day 326   November 21

WHEN TIMES ARE wonderful, we tend to wander from God, and sadly, this is what has happened in our country... We have lived in the beautiful freedom of America, and yet there are those who hate this country, burn our flag, and threaten to leave when things don't go their way... My prayer is that we learn the easy way because "the wise man learns by watching while a fool has to have a rod taken to his back." I pray that God's continued mercy and grace will smile on our homeland and that we will be grateful in all things.

UNDER ALL CIRCUMSTANCES, keep your concern and focus on men. Disruptions in life are inevitable but always remember that people and their safety and well-being are what matter most. Money and material things are always secondary. "Love others as you love yourself."

Day 327 — November 22

"I WILL GO before you and make the rough places smooth." Yet many times, we can clearly see our path is scattered with all sorts of bumps and potholes... These fiery trials are all part of the process... This does not mean that you should not proceed... "Count it all joy when you go through the fiery trials because it is perfecting you." "Fire refines you just as it does gold and silver." The iron that has been through the fire is the strongest!

PRAYER MAKES THE difference. There are times that you pray, and it seems as though God did not hear you, but "God's ears are open to your prayers." Even though it may not immediately manifest itself, He hears your prayer the moment you pray. Even though the answer may be delayed... it will come to pass if you do not waver. "He who wavers gets nothing from God."

Day 328 — November 23

A CHRISTIAN IS not necessarily a disciple of Jesus... The word "Christian" is thrown around as if it is so easy to be one just by calling yourself such... But the truth is that much more is required to become a true disciple of Jesus... A disciple must give their total allegiance to Jesus and must live a disciplined life as we teach and propagate His teachings... "You must love me with all your heart, all your soul, and all your mind." And the best part of this is: "Those who put their trust in Jesus will never be disappointed."

SURROUND YOURSELF WITH things that make you happy. You have the ability to change your environment. It doesn't take money or material things—just an attitude of gratitude, a little elbow grease, and creative thinking as you refresh your surroundings. If you make the most of what you already have, I promise you, God will bring increase. Sitting around whining and wallowing in self-pity will only deepen the pit. *"If you're faithful with a little, you will receive much."*

Day 329 — November 24

"GOD KNOWS YOUR name even before you were born," and you can imagine His sorrow as abortion snuffs out this life that God has already named... God gives us the right to choose, and He will allow us to choose to abort a baby, just as He allows mankind to choose all sorts of things that grieve Him and bring curses upon us... and He will never take away the right to choose... "I lay before you, life and death, blessing and cursing; choose life."

BE CAREFUL THAT we do not become so familiar in our relationship with Jesus that we lose our awe and amazement of God. "The fear of God is the beginning of wisdom." And fear is simply respect! Yes, He is our Daddy, our Provider, and our Savior, but He still holds a huge standard in our lives. Our God is omnipotent... Never take this lightly! "Love God with all your heart, all your soul, all your might, and all your strength."

Day 330 — November 25

A PERSON WITH an experience is never at the mercy of an argument... When you share your experience, there cannot be an argument... Just share what you have seen and heard, and let others do what they will with your knowledge... Your own personal experience is your witness to others... "We overcome the enemy by the blood of the Lamb and the word of our testimony."

TRIALS CAN AFFECT us spiritually, physically, and emotionally, and life is full of trials. Keep in mind that these trials always come with "hidden treasures in dark secret places." Be determined to find the treasures that are hidden within. "Count it all joy when you go through fiery trials because it is perfecting you."

Day 331   November 26

EINSTEIN ONCE SAID, "Life is like riding a bicycle. You have to keep moving to keep your balance," and this is so true... As you move through life, God promises to "direct your steps." God cannot direct your steps if you're not moving... No matter what happens in your life, keep going. "As you forget the things that are behind and look towards the things that are ahead..."

"IN ACCEPTANCE LIES peace." Do not run away from things... Stand and face your issues... If you run, they will follow you, and you'll have to deal with them again. And don't bury them either by pretending they're not there... They will only surface again in some other way. Embrace what is going on and move through it as easily and efficiently as you can. Ask God to help as He "directs your steps as you go."

Day 332 — November 27

"LET THERE BE light." The spoken words of God created physical light to brighten a dark world... When we speak God's Word, we are bringing light into a dark situation... And remember that "darkness cannot be where there is light." Learn God's Word so you can use it to brighten a life, and in so doing, you brighten your own life... "God's Word never comes back void; it always does what it set out to do."

GOD'S WORD IS fluid and timeless. "It is the same yesterday, today, and forever." Regardless of the internet, Google, or AI that is constantly changing... the Word of God never changes. Your ancestry, all the way back, read the same book, and it was just as relevant then as it is today. The Bible has the answer to absolutely everything... It is your life book of instructions. "Study to make yourself approved."

Day 333   November 28

WHEN YOU ARE grateful, you open the spiritual gifts of Heaven... Take the time to verbally say thank you to God for all your blessings... Those who are grateful will always find new blessings flowing their way... The ungrateful will not even notice or be able to enjoy their blessings... Gratefulness is one of the finest gifts you can have... As you enjoy your family and your food today: "In everything, give thanks."

MORE PEOPLE WALK away from God during tragedy than at any other time, and this is when we really need Him. Press into God during troubles because this is the time that you can grow the closest to Him and see His miracles come to pass in your life. "God is made strongest in your weakness."

Day 334   November 29

UNTIL YOU HAVE made Jesus the Lord of your life, you will not be able to understand the Word of God... Even well-educated people find the Bible perplexing and unbelievable if Jesus is not their Lord... It is filled with parables and hidden treasures that are given only to believers... "Seeing they do not see, and hearing they do not hear, nor do they understand." "To you, it has been given to know the secrets of the kingdom of Heaven, but to them, it has not been given."

GOD OFTEN USES dreams to talk to us. Pay attention to your dreams and try to glean from them. "God knows your dreams and your plans." Sometimes dreams are nothing more than your mind going over things that have happened in the past... or a way of purging you of anger or disappointment... Throughout the Bible, God used dreams, visions, and interpretations to warn, instruct, and help His people.

Day 335 — November 30

YOU ARE CONSTANTLY evolving... You are not who you were last year, last month, or even yesterday... The changes are sometimes small and almost indistinguishable but real nonetheless... Earnestly seek Godly wisdom in every circumstance as you continue to grow... "We are the clay, and You are our potter; and all we are the work of Your hand."

WHEN WE ARE born, we tend to look like our parents and our family... But when we die, we will look like our choices. Choices make a difference in every single area of life, including the way you look. Remember that everything you keep in your head will eventually show up on your face. Bad choices will always cause those who make them to look ugly. "God lays before us life and death, blessing and cursing. Choose life." Choose well.

Greg was Such a good boy right from the start,
Easy to raise and a precious little heart ...
A straight 'A' student and athletic as well,
Success in his future, it was easy to tell...
All the girls loved him and their mothers too,
He was a catch and this everyone knew...
But it was Monica Rickert who won his heart,
She picked him out right from the start...
His choice of Monica was the right one,
With 2 daughters and their amazing son...
The years have gone and it's a blessing to see,
The kind of man that Greg Solis would be...
A Godly man without a doubt,
Trustworthy and honest is what he's about...
Whatever he does, he's ahead of the pack,
In every area of life, there's no visible lack...
At the start of each year, his goals are set,
And he doesn't quit until every goal is met...
His mother just couldn't be any more blessed,
Though in his youth, she put him to the test...
Thank you, Greg for the person you've become,
I am so very proud; You're a wonderful son...

– Velma Hagar for Greg Solis, Son

December

Day 336   December 1

SOMETIMES YOU HAVE to build yourself up... When you feel low or things are not going well, remind yourself of who you are in the Lord... You are a child of God, and you have unique abilities that only you can perform in this life... Choose to believe the best about yourself and your capabilities... "Build yourself up in the Holy Spirit."

REBELLION WILL ALWAYS lead to disaster. Humble yourself and let go of rebellion and disobedience to God's word. "If you will draw close to God, He will draw close to you." Always choose to do the right thing. I firmly believe that God built into us the knowledge of what is right, and there is a scripture in the Bible that will cover absolutely anything that you need. Before you make any foolish choices, find a scripture that will either confirm or negate your decision before moving forward. Foolish choices will cause you to crash. "Those who put their faith in God will never be disappointed."

Day 337   December 2

"THE FRUIT OF the Spirit is love, joy, peace, patience, kindness, goodness, faithfulness, gentleness, and self-control." It is true that most of us struggle to maintain all of these sweet character traits, but as you continue to walk in the Spirit, you will find these things will come easier to you… "Walk in the Spirit, and you will not gratify the desires of the flesh."

GOD HAS A purpose for everyone. You are not intended to just envy or try to mimic others. You are beautiful in your own right. Press into who you are as you grab hold of your assets and manage your weaknesses. We all have weaknesses that need to be managed and assets that need to be appreciated. God has a specific purpose for your life. "You are wondrously made," and "God is faithful to finish the work He has started in you."

Day 338 — December 3

THERE ARE MOMENTS in your life that will determine your destiny... Sometimes it's one minor change that trumps everything else that was done before... One decision, and everything familiar can be gone... One unguarded moment can destroy a life... Do not become a victim to the temptations that surround us every day... "The enemy roams around like a lion seeking whom he may destroy"... "Seek first the kingdom of God and His righteousness, and all other things will be added."

THERE IS NOTHING that you've ever done that cannot be fixed... Absolutely nothing! Our God is so forgiving and gracious that all it takes is a sincere "I'm sorry," and if you really mean it, you have a fresh start. Don't we wish that men were as gracious? "I will forgive their iniquities, and I will remember their sins no more." A complete clean slate! Ask God to forgive you, then turn from any unacceptable ways and begin a fresh journey.

Day 339 — December 4

NOT EVERY BEAUTIFUL thing that comes to you in your life is from God... The enemy has the ability to offer worldly goods to people... But God says, "Unless God builds the house, they that labor, labor in vain." Never accept anything that you do not believe is from God... Remember that the blessings from above are "pure and peaceful."

DECLARATIONS ARE SO important, and even in the face of deep, dark days, they are more important than ever. No matter what happens to you, declare out loud the things that you know to be true. Your "words have the power of life and death in them." A positive, fervent declaration is like adding fertilizer to a plant, while negative words can destroy.

Day 340   December 5

JUST BECAUSE A sin has been legalized does not mean it is not a sin... Neither the government nor anyone else has the right to change God's laws... We are told in the scriptures to "Obey the laws of the land." This does not mean that the laws of the land supersede God's word... As a Christian, we are to obey all of God's rules, even if the land we live in chooses to ignore God... Walk as straight a line as you can, because this keeps you on a "Holy Highway where no evil things may travel."

THE REALITY OF life is that many times we cannot see the purpose of what is happening in our lives, and we cannot even begin to imagine how this could possibly work toward good, as God promises. But if you will simply trust God and proclaim God's promise about your issue... at the last, you will see your redemption. Stand and believe. "All things work together for good to those who believe and love God and are called according to His purpose for them."

Day 341 — December 6

THE BATTLES IN life almost always start with your eyes... You see something and you want it, and many times you get it without waiting for God... "Keep your eyes on the things above and not on the things below." Always take the time to ask God for what you desire, because He monitors what is best for you... Not everything you desire is good for you... "Seek first the kingdom of God and His righteousness, and everything else will be added."

WHEN YOU ARE in a place of weakness, you are also in a place to receive a miracle. We all love miracles, and yet miracles usually only happen during times of great stress. Ask God for a miracle, and then expect God to do something big in your life. "As you believe, it is done unto you." And stop talking negatively about your situation! Call out what you want to have happen, and then stand and believe.

Day 342

December 7

"IN YOUR WEAKNESS God is made strong." When you are feeling helpless or inadequate, this is the very time that you can get to know how powerful God is... He is never stronger in our lives than when we are feeling weak... The old adage that says "Let go and let God" has a lot of merit. Do you feel like you can't do it? Try letting go and letting God.

CALL OUT WHAT you know to be true even when life is overwhelming. Remind God of His promises. "Bring Me in remembrance of My Word." God actually tells us to remind Him of the promises that He has made to us, and yet I rarely hear people do that! What the heck? "You have not because you ask not." God has made a provision for everything you need. Read the Bible, find your promise, and remind God of it...

Day 343 — December 8

"TASTE AND SEE that the Lord is good." I want to tell you folks that I have tasted and I have seen how absolutely wonderful my God is... I literally feel so sorry for people who have never known the love of the Father like I do... As I watch all of my friends aging and see the trials of the flesh as it wanes, I am even more aware of how much we need the promises that are given to the children of God... I want to tell you folks... My old age is wonderful! It is truly golden! Not that I don't have all the issues that everybody else has, because I do... But my heart and my spirit are soaring as I think of how close I'm getting to being home with my Heavenly Father... I am happy... full of a zest for life (though my body resists a little), and I'm going to savor every precious moment that I have left in this life. And my prayer for you this holiday season is that you too will come to know your Father in Heaven like I do... In Jesus' name.

A FAITHFUL PERSON will always be blessed. If we only asked God for one attribute, it should be faithfulness. The coveted words upon seeing Jesus are "Well done, good and faithful servant." To be loyal and steadfast is truly what pleases our God.

Day 344 — December 9

GODLINESS IS A mystery... It cannot be truly understood until you actually experience it... Even the scriptures in the Bible are mysterious to the unbeliever... "The wisdom of the world is foolishness to those who are perishing." and the wisdom of man is foolishness to God... There is nothing sweeter than the pleasant surprise of understanding the mysteries of God...

"THE HOLY SPIRIT enables us to witness to others. It also "tells us things we do not know." There are nine gifts of the Spirit. Be bold when you feel a prompting to pray, teach, lay on hands for healing, help, encourage, prophesy, and so forth. These are the gifts of the Spirit, and all of us are blessed with all nine gifts, even though we may find ourselves extraordinarily gifted in one or two. Be available to God to use you wherever He chooses."

Day 345   December 10

CHRISTMAS IS SO much more than celebrating the birth of Jesus... It is pretty certain that Dec. 25th is not really the day Jesus was born, but it is a great celebration of His birth regardless of the date... Enjoy the celebrations but stay mindful of the profundity of this miracle... "God so loved the world that He gave His only Son, that whoever believes in Him shall not perish, but have eternal life."

IF YOU HAVE a plan... Go forward with gusto, even if there is a better plan that may manifest itself later. Do what you know to do today as you keep your hands moving, and "God will direct your steps as you go." Any plan today is better than a possible plan tomorrow. Sometimes, if you just keep moving, you will bumble into it.

Day 346   December 11

THE NUMBER ONE fear in life is rejection, and the number one need is acceptance. These two issues are what propel people through life. Unfortunately, the need to be accepted often pushes others away when one cares too much. People are fickle, and you can't always count on them. But when you really get to know your Savior, the need to be accepted by men becomes a lot less. God promises that "He will never leave you nor forsake you."

GOD WILL USE the conflicts and chaos in your life to connect with you. He can use your chaotic life to shine His light through you. Chaos causes fatigue, so a chaotic life often leads to feelings of despair and deep-down tiredness. "Seek first the kingdom of God and His righteousness, and all other things will be added to you."

Day 347 — December 12

EVERYTHING THAT YOU say out of your mouth is what you are claiming for yourself. Every time you say something negative about life or yourself, you are claiming that. Always reach out and grab those things that are said that you want in your life. Claim them for yourself just as you would physically take a gift that was offered to you. In the spirit realm, these things are very real. "Call things that are not as though they are." You shall only have what you say—nothing more.

JESUS PROMISES US that He will "give us the peace that goes beyond understanding, not like the world gives" with pills or years of counseling as you share the mean things over and over that your mommy and daddy did to you when you were little. It is an inner peace that permeates your life, and circumstances do not affect your peace. Remind God of this wonderful promise.

DAY 348   December 13

GOD BLESSES EVERYONE the same at the beginning of life; however, blessings can be lost because of the choices we make. God is never the one that pulls away from us, but when choices are made to step outside of God's principles, we pull away from God, and blessings are lost. "Draw close to Him, and He will draw close to you."

GOD'S WORD TELLS us that in the end times, "knowledge will increase." Today, our universities and colleges are filled with scholarly knowledge but totally lack any idea of who God is or even logical reasoning. Twenty-three percent of students actually feel that the Bible should be outlawed because it contains hate speech! Please pray for our youth because they are going to be the leaders of tomorrow—a scary thought for sure.

Day 349 — December 14

"IT IS A sin to do what you know you ought to do and then not do it." As Christians, we are told that "there is therefore no condemnation to him who is in Christ Jesus," but this is not a carte blanche to sin. We are still held responsible for what we know. In fact, "the more you know, the more that is expected of you."

LET BYGONES BE bygones. There is never a good reason to hang on to unforgiveness. Life is full of all sorts of mishaps and misgivings, and the sooner we can release these from our lives, the easier life will be. We all make mistakes, and just as Jesus said, "He will remember your sin no more" once you've asked for forgiveness, we should extend the same mercy to others. Remember, "if you don't forgive others, God will not forgive you."

DAY 350   December 15

"I WOULD HAVE lost heart unless I had believed that I would see the goodness of the Lord in the land of the living." Life is troubled, but God is very visible in the midst of that trouble. Look for the goodness of God, and remember that what your eyes see is very important. You can choose to see the troubled world or the goodness of God. We all know my choice.

GOD TELLS US to "bring Him in remembrance of His word," not because He doesn't know what it says, but because He wants us to know what it says! If you have a need, find the promise that covers that need and remind God of what He said. If you haven't read the Bible and don't know what the promises are, it's like not claiming your inheritance. The principles of God are for everyone, but the promises can only be claimed by those who call Him Lord.

Day 351   December 16

"PRAY ONE FOR the other that you might be healed." Every time you pray for someone else, you are actually praying for yourself as well! I have made a commitment to pray for anyone who asks for prayer, whether I know them or not, and then I remind God of what He promises. We need to do it the way God tells us to do it. Pray for others and then "bring Him in remembrance of His word."

WHEN YOU SAY yes to something, you are also saying no to many other things. Your time is a precious commodity, and it seems that time is racing by. Choose the things that you are going to say yes to. You can't do everything, and when you try, you subtract from the things that really matter. "There is a time and a season for everything under the sun." Don't try to do it all in one day.

Day 352 — December 17

"PURSUE PEACE WITH all due diligence." If there are those in your life who rob you of your joy and peace, separate yourself from them because "we have been called to a life of peace." Troubles do exist, but we should always have peace, even in the midst of our trials. If you do not have that peace, something is out of order. Ask God to show you what it is, and then make the necessary changes. "God gives us a peace that goes beyond understanding."

GOD SAYS "I will finish the work I have started in you." What is it about us that wants to fix people? We all do it... And yet many times all that is needed Is someone to come along side of us and hear us out and be our friend without any judgment or counseling... there is nothing sweeter than a friend that listens. "It is not good for man to be alone because when he falls, there's no one to pick him up."

Day 353 — December 18

"GOD DELIGHTS IN the prayers of His people." Never think that God is too busy to listen to your prayer! He is omnipotent, and He can hear and do everything. "You have not because you ask not." Do not complain about things if you haven't even taken the time to pray. Prayer works! Find a trusted friend, get into agreement about your needs, and then let God handle His part.

HAVE YOU EVER wondered where God is? There are times when it seems that everyone else is getting blessed, yet God doesn't seem to hear your prayers. We know that God is invisible, but though we cannot see Him, His presence can be felt and heard in our spirit, and we can see His fingerprint everywhere we look. And yet, sometimes it seems He eludes us. But be assured that "God will never leave you nor forsake you." Never give up on God. "In due season, you shall have your reward."

Day 354   December 19

THE BOOK OF Acts is the beginning of the transition from the Old to the New Testament. Remember that the Old Testament is still active in our lives; the only change is that we do not have to do the sacrifices anymore because Jesus was the sacrifice. We are no longer under the law, and we now have the Holy Spirit. But always remember that the whole Bible "is the same yesterday, today, and tomorrow." Read the Bible from beginning to end and find all the wonderful "hidden treasures" within.

DON'T JUST GRIEVE what you have lost, but embrace what you have left. God will always replace what you have lost, but many times we spend so much time grieving our losses that we miss the joy of the replacement. Take note of what God has given and "give thanks in everything."

Day 355 — December 20

OPEN FOR ME the gates where the righteous may enter, and I will go in and thank the Lord. These special gates lead to the presence of the Lord, and only the godly are allowed to go there. I love to call this my holy highway, where no evil thing may travel. You cannot imagine the joy of knowing the Lord as I do. "Draw close to Him, and He will draw close to you." There's nothing finer in this life.

GOD'S WORD SAYS, "Pray one for the other that you might be healed." I stand on that scripture every day of my life because, as most of you know, I have a prayer ministry. And now I need you to pray for me. I woke up this morning all plugged up, achy, and weak. I'm doing everything I need to do to pamper myself, and I also know that every time I ever get sick, when it passes over, there are some beautiful life changes that happen. Thank you.

Day 356 — December 21

"THEREFORE, DO NOT worry about tomorrow, for tomorrow will worry about its own things. Sufficient for the day is its own trouble." Wouldn't it be grand if all of us could operate like this? Every one of us tends to worry about tomorrow, and the Bible actually says, "Fret not, because it will only cause harm." Bring this scripture to mind every time you find yourself fretting about tomorrow...

THE FEAR OF God is described as awe and intimacy. Always maintain reverence for God just as you would a strict, loving father. Never become so familiar with the grace of God that you lose your fear and respect. God is omnipotent, and it is only His grace and mercy that protect us. "Love the Lord with all your heart, soul, and all your strength and mind."

Day 357 — December 22

YOUR SECURITY LIES in doing God's will... "Obedience is better than sacrifice." When you have chosen to do things God's way, no matter what comes at you, you will be rescued by God... Honor God, and you can rest assured that He will always take care of you... What an amazing promise.

GO THE EXTRA mile. Stretch your love and your servitude just a little more. It is similar to exercising a muscle—every time you stretch a muscle, it gets bigger and more flexible, and it gets easier to stretch the next time. God says, "Above all, love each other deeply." Do everything you know to do with what you have for as long as you can.

Day 358   December 23

SANTA CLAUS IS often looked down on by the legalistic religious folk... But the truth is that he is the embodiment of everything Jesus wants us to be... Loving, kind, and giving... As a child, Santa was my hero... He is in no way a god, but he brings a mystical magic to childhood, and I love him. "The eye is the lamp of the body. If your eye is healthy, your whole body is full of light..."

WHEN YOU LOVE God, everything else will flow from that. "Seek first the kingdom of God and His righteousness, and all other things will be added to you." When you keep God at the head of your life, everything else will fall into place. When you find yourself fragmented and overwhelmed, check and be sure that God is still your pilot.

Day 359 — December 24

I WILL GIVE you the treasures of darkness and the things hidden in secret places." There are so many things that we do not see with our eyes... Treasures, blessings, beauty everywhere, and yet we stumble over them many times and miss them... Ask God to show you those hidden treasures in dark secret places... Then be expectant... Merry Christmas.

WHATEVER YOU THINK about, you bring about. Thoughts are not harmless. If you allow things to stay in your head, they will eventually manifest into reality. We can't stop a thought from coming, but we can stop it from finding a home in our head. God tells us to "cast down wild imaginings and any thought that exalts itself above God's word." Your thoughts are blueprints for your life. They matter.

Day 360 — December 25

THERE IS AN old adage that says, "A family that prays together stays together." This is a picture of our enormous family taken a few years ago at Christmas time... As you can see, we have grown to a group that is so large that when we include all of our new babies, it is almost impossible to get together in one house. But our prayers, though sometimes in different places, are still for each other... This picture was the last time our brother Bob was with us at Christmas... The years have gone by, and we've certainly grown from that poor little struggling Hagar clan, but the heart of the family is intact. I encourage all of you to pray together and pray for one another... Create memories that will never be forgotten, and remember to include Jesus, who is the real reason for the season... Merry Christmas to all...

AS WE POLISH off the year, find a wonderful scripture that you want to activate in your life for the new year. Set a goal to grow in God's word. As for me, I have asked God to give me more compassion for those who think differently than I do and to truly "consider the other more important than myself." Now, how about you? What is your goal?

Day 361   December 26

BE REAL... DO not sugarcoat or exaggerate things, and don't sweep them under the rug either... Be a trustworthy person of integrity who is willing to embrace the things you have done wrong and always tells the truth without exaggeration... "The Lord detests lying lips, but He delights in those who are trustworthy..."

AND JUST AS you want men to do to you, you also do to them likewise." Your treatment of others will determine how life will treat you. "Be not deceived... As you sow, you shall reap." Every single thing that you do to others will come back on you in one way or another... So be nice if you want life to be nice to you.

Day 362   December 27

LIFE WITH ALL of its ups and downs has created a beautiful tapestry of your life... A colorful, intricate quilt, so to speak... A unique, one-of-a-kind piece... And the more experiences in your life, the more beautiful and valuable the tapestry is... There is no other quilt exactly like yours. "God has a plan for your life, and it's a good plan... A plan to prosper you and not to harm you..."

LET US THEN with confidence draw near to the throne of grace, that we may receive mercy and find grace to help in time of need." It always amazes me when people say things like, "I don't ask God for help; He's got better things to do." Duh!!! Our God is omnipotent, and He can do everything at once... Always ask... "You have not because you ask not."

Day 363 — December 28

THE BIBLE IS filled with all sorts of twists, turns, and surprises... It is like fluid as it fills every nook and cranny of our life... "It is the same yesterday, today, and tomorrow," and yet every time you read it, you find something different... It seems to change as we change... We hear and see what we need to hear and see... There is a promise for every need, and it warns of every pitfall in life... A beautiful book of instruction and inspiration... "Study to make yourself approved..."

THE BIGGER THE problem, the greater the triumph. Little problem... little triumph... Big problem... big triumph. My dad, who was a professional boxer, used to say, "The bigger they are, the harder they fall." And you know it's true... The more we have to overcome, the more treasures will come out of the battle. It may seem that some things are too big for you, but always remember, "I can do all things through Christ, who strengthens me."

Day 364 — December 29

A JUDGMENT AND an observation are totally different, though many times we can manipulate a judgment and make it appear to be an observation… "A wise man learns by watching" is referring to an observation… But care needs to be observed at these times, because it is so easy to even fool ourselves, and a judgment brings a curse down on us… "As you judge, you will be judged." CAREFUL!!!

LIVE YOUR LIFE in such a way that when people think of integrity, they think of you. It doesn't matter how others act; it is our place to always do what is right… God built it into us to know instinctively right from wrong, and it is our responsibility as God's children to display integrity in every area of life. The simplicity of God's requirement of us is "to act justly, love mercy, and to walk humbly before our God."

Day 365 — December 30

WHERE YOUR TREASURES lie, there will be your heart also." Treasures are not always tangible... Your faith and your relationship with the Lord are a wealth of treasure... All the gold and silver in the world cannot make up for a lost spiritual life with God... Never think of yourself as poor if you have a personal relationship with your Father in Heaven... "Do not store up treasures on earth, where moths and vermin destroy and where thieves break in and steal... Store your treasures in the safety of the spiritual realm with God..."

THERE IS POWER in one moment... One moment can change your life. There are moments in your life that determine your destiny and moments that will determine your life. Be cautious that you don't let the temptation of one weak moment destroy your life. Always be aware that "your adversary sneaks around like a roaring lion, seeking whom he may destroy."

Day 366 — December 31

NEVER KEEP AN offense in your craw... It can stay there for years, and it will affect your relationship with who brought about the offense... You may think you have forgiven them, and you still have a relationship with them, but you have never discussed the thing they did that hurt you... If it is in your craw, you have not totally forgiven them... "Forgive that you may be forgiven"... Get your heart right and then communicate...

WHAT IS IT about mankind that keeps doing the same thing over and over when it's not working? The old adage that says "don't ride a dead horse" has a lot of merit to it. I think every one of us is guilty... Sometimes there's a fine line between persevering and being stuck in the past. "Forgetting the things that are behind and looking towards the things that are ahead." Look for the new thing in the new year.

www.ingramcontent.com/pod-product-compliance
Lightning Source LLC
Chambersburg PA
CBHW020415010526
44118CB00010B/266